Complete and Magical Guide to Dog Training and Parenting

The Most Important, Powerful, Successful Puppy Training Advice, Secrets, Tips, and Tricks You Need to Know to Raise Perfect Dogs

J.J. Wallace

losses, direct or indirect, that are incurred as a result of the use of the information contained within this document, including, but not limited to, errors, omissions, or inaccuracies.

Table of Contents

Introduction

"When it comes to training a dog, 5 minutes a day Monday through Friday is better than 30 minutes on Saturday." (Deeley, 2020b)

Congratulations on your decision to bring a fur baby into your home. This quote above sums up consistency in training. That is key when you are bringing a new pet into your surroundings. I have some wonderful and easy training methods to guide you, and you will be surprised at the progress you will make in such a short time.

This help guide will assist you in avoiding all the mistakes and stress. It is tried and tested positive reinforcements that are connected to corrective techniques and methods for your benefit. I will walk you through the various steps that are required to successfully raise your pup into a well-behaved and socialized pet.

I will be providing you with all of the information you need to best care for your pet. There is a reason why dogs are known to be man's best friend; they are loving animals who enjoy making new friends. Your new family member will imprint on all the hearts that surround it.

Unlike humans, every dog is unique, and personalities can differ, even in the same breed. If you are looking for a dog who will be excited to join your pack, you need to make sure of your choice.

I am here to help you choose and match the best fur baby to your individual personality and lifestyle. This will have no bearing on the first dog or another in a long line of family pets, or whether you are looking for an older rescue or a purebred puppy.

Dogs come in all shapes and sizes, from teacup poodles to Saint Bernards. Small dog breeds are generally easier to care for but they have problems of their own to deal with. The tiny tots, however, make a popular choice for dog owners who live in smaller homes.

If you want to buy or adopt a large dog, you should carefully weigh the benefits and drawbacks before bringing one home. Both purebred and mixed breed dogs have advantages and disadvantages, and you will never bring any fur member home that is perfect.

What kind of dog you get, however, is entirely dependent on your requirements and should be a personal choice. Before you adopt, make a list of your wants, needs, and expectations, and discuss them with the rest of your family. This will assist you in making the right decision and finding the ideal fur baby for you. So, let's get started!

Chapter 1:
Which Dog Is Right for You?

"Before you get a dog, you can't quite imagine what living with one might be like; afterward, you can't imagine living any other way." (Knapp, 2010)

This quote is so accurate, and I speak from personal experience. I can't imagine our life without the love and playfulness of our fur babies. It is important to find the right match in the beginning so that everyone will be happy, including your fur child, when it arrives.

I have set out a few questions and answers to help you to decide which dog is best suited to your lifestyle and if you have the time and patience for the responsibility it takes. Keep in mind that if you are looking for a puppy, a prospective breeder may ask you these questions to determine whether your home is suitable for one of their puppies.

Questions to Ask Yourself

Can I Give Enough Attention to a Dog?

One of the most important questions to ask yourself is whether you have enough time for a dog. When we plan for a family, this question is researched extensively. This should be the same when you are adopting a dog. A dog is an addition to the family, and all the members of the family should feel excited and want to spend time with the furry addition. Each dog is different and, even in a certain breed, they can vary.

An animal that is confident and keeps itself busy would probably only need 30 minutes to an hour a day of intensive exercise. This would include a bit of one on one time in general for most breeds. Other dog owners may disagree and state that 1 to 2 hours should be set aside and dedicated to a dog.

My suggestion is that you should analyze your lifestyle; if you love the outdoors and love to run and hike, play sports, and interact with other dog owners, or you have family on farms, I would suggest a high-energy breed like a pointer, border Collie, Australian cattle dog, or a mixed breed that is energetic, as they require a lot more time and effort to exert all of their energy.

Dogs are pack-type animals, and they need love and attention. Life can't stop, and we have to be realistic as it can't revolve around your pup either. It's also difficult to budget time spent on your fur baby each day. A dog is a commitment, so time, caring, loving, and the welfare of your animal are very important.

However, in saying that, too much time spent with your dog can result in separation anxiety and this is detected in certain events, such as leaving your pup to go to town or visit a friend. An unhealthy dependence occurs, and the animal becomes extremely stressed and emotional whenever you are separated from it.

Pets should be trained and comfortable in their space, so they will accept an owner leaving the house for a certain time frame. There are always exceptions to the rule, for instance, animals, such as seeing-eye dogs, are trained as guide dogs for visually-impaired people, as well as police dogs. These types of dogs have extensive training and can't be categorized in the same bracket.

If you are concerned about the time you have to spend or if you already have an animal at home, and you are looking for answers, find yourself the right doggie daycare and try it out for a while. When your fur baby is jumping for joy, as your doggie realizes it's that time again and it can't wait to leave and get out of the car on arriving at the daycare, you will know you have struck it right.

Am I Patient Enough?

All animals need patience and will only learn if you don't appear angry and threatening. Consider life through the eyes of your fur baby, as they only have a hazy understanding of what you are asking of it in the first place. The environment is new and still perplexing, and they don't have that much control over their behavior.

If you respond in a loud, angry voice or rough treatment, they will be less inclined to trust you or react favorably. Trying to teach your pup house-training, sleeping through the night, not to bite or chew, and all the other domestic rules that you have established, all at once, can become overwhelming.

It is good to consider a puppy's sense of curiosity, energy, and wonder. Both of you are learning; perhaps your fur animal is eager to impress you and understand what is required of them, but you should be patient, calm, and consistent.

Dogs are sensitive to their owner's moods. If you are anxious, stressed, frustrated, or impatient, your fur member will pick it up. This will make the learning process even more difficult to teach and communicate.

If you find yourself frustrated or starting to lose your patience, take a deep breath and follow a few simple guidelines that I will give you to get back on track.

If you have other members in your family, you could take turns when you have had a difficult day. Alternatively, you can place your fur bundle gently in its crate or a gated area and take some time to relax and calm down.

It is important to understand a breed's temperament and behavioral characteristics. If you've done your research into your adopted breed, you will find its traits are easier to work with rather than against its natural tendencies.

Spending as much time as possible with your puppy will build a bond and trust, making it easier for them to understand your expectations, and this may also reduce your frustration level.

Practice makes perfect, and every animal is similar to a child. They might not understand what you are teaching them for the first or fifth time. Just remember that some may catch on rather quickly. By giving them a chance to succeed and being patient and consistent, they will eventually get it. Don't forget to compliment them, even with minor victories.

Introducing an adorable bundle of energy into your household changes your life in the most unexpected ways. Remember that you are attempting to teach it good habits for life, which won't happen overnight.

How Much Does It Cost?

You have probably heard that dogs are pricey. I am not going to deceive you, this rumor is accurate. Dog care requires investment. It is better to understand the specifics of dog care costs upfront. They are not one-time expenses, there can be monthly expenses, and even annual expenses to consider. It's all relative to choices made in animals, healthcare, and luxuries, so there are ways to save money.

The cost of owning a dog extends beyond the cost of food. Unfortunately, many people walk into dog ownership blindly, and they don't make the effort to budget for a dog before purchasing one, which can lead to problems later on.

Before you get a dog, plan and learn where your limits are. Being responsible includes financially providing for your dogs. The annual cost of owning a dog can range anywhere between $1,500 and $9,900. Your dog's size and age, the region in which you live, your lifestyle, and your dog's individual needs are all factors.

Should You Get a Puppy or an Adult Dog?

Considering puppies are a lot of work, when you bring a puppy home, you should expect to miss out on your regular amount of sleep due to puppies missing their littermates and crying at night due to separation anxiety. Puppies and small dogs have small bladders. They can't keep it in all night and will need to go potty once or several times during your sleeping time.

Being exhausted from being up all night with a puppy who just wants to play can be difficult to accept. It could take from a few weeks to six months for one puppy to stop waking you up at night. Some pet owners sleep with their puppy until they are about six months old.

I don't want to scare you too much, but some dogs need to potty at night until they are a year old. In these cases, consider ending eating and drinking habits earlier at night.

Whether or not you are a late sleeper, you will need to work on training your puppy to be one as well. If you purchase a dog from a pet store, online seller, or flea market, make certain that you are not purchasing a puppy from a puppy mill.

Puppy mills are production plant breeding facilities that prioritize profit over dogs' welfare. Puppy mill animals are treated shockingly and live in poor conditions with inadequate medical care, and as a result, they are frequently very sick and behaviorally troubled.

These puppies' mothers are kept in cages for years, without human companionship and with little hope of ever joining a family. When breeding dogs are no longer profitable, they are simply discarded; either abandoned, killed, or auctioned off.

These puppy mills remain in business by using deceptive tactics, and they are often sold to unexpecting customers. I am afraid to say that puppy mills will exist until people stop supporting them.

Benefits of older dogs

Puppy love is universal, I get it. Puppies are so cute and cuddly. It stands to reason that when looking for a new dog, the younger, the better. However, you may be surprised at how rewarding adopting an older dog can be. However, adopting a pet will ensure that you are not wasting your money.

Every year, it is estimated that over one million dogs waiting to be adopted are euthanized in the United States, as there are too many animals in shelters with too few people considering adoption (ASPCA, 2021).

The number of animals put to sleep may be reduced significantly if more people choose to adopt pets rather than buy them. Adopting a dog or cat allows you to save a devoted creature by including them in your family and frees up shelter space for another needy animal.

Animal shelters and rescue organizations are teeming with happy, healthy pets just waiting for a new home. Most pets end up in a shelter due to issues, such as their owner's death, moving, divorce, or simply them being too much work. A lot of these animals have nothing wrong with them, and many of them are already house trained and accustomed to living with families.

When you adopt a pet, most of the costs have already been taken care of. This includes sterilization, first vaccinations, and sometimes microchipping. This would all be included in the adoption fee. This saves money on the initial costs of adding a new member to your family.

Depending on the animal, you could also save money, certain breeds are prone to health problems, and this should also be considered. An older dog often realizes that you have saved them from a situation, and they can be extremely loveable and eager to please.

You may have a couple of issues to work on but, on the whole, they are a far easier option as their temperament is a lot calmer, and you can see what you have in a dog far easier than a puppy.

Size of Dog

Small Dog Considerations

Dogs weighing approximately 30 pounds or less are considered small dogs. Small-breed dogs seem to be perfectly suited in condos and apartments, as they don't overpower the furniture and are easier to lift and carry in the event of illness or injury. One thing I've noticed is there are a set of difficulties that come with a small dog:

The standard space between banister or railing spindles is wide enough for smaller canines to fit through. So, never leave a small dog alone on a deck, boat loft, or balcony. Small dogs should avoid these areas as they can easily jump or fall. Small dogs can get stuck in areas they have explored, and they can be lost at times.

Some smaller fluffs have alpha personalities, but others are bullied by larger pets. As comical as it may seem when your cat overpowers your small dog, it's no laughing matter if the aggressor begins to regard your vulnerable canine as lunch.

Remember that at dog parks, small puppies can become the target of dangerous predator behavior and are susceptible to attack from animals, such as hawks and coyotes. Small dogs, however, will always have enough space and are often budget-friendly, as everything that is bought for them comes in a smaller size.

Medium Dog Considerations

Medium dogs have a wide range of body weights. To make it easier to specify the exact size of dog you're looking for. There are three distinct groups of medium-sized dogs:

- Medium small: Standard dachshunds, French bulldogs, and corgis
- Medium: Beagles and border collies

- Medium to large: Shar-peis, samoyeds and many female dogs from larger breeds are medium sizes, such as Airedale terriers and poodles

Medium-sized dog breeds are the goldilocks of dogs, as they are neither too big nor too small for several prospective pet parents. This size of dog is the most popular as it has a little of both worlds in one. Temperaments and characteristics vary as much as their sizes do. Medium-sized dog breeds in general offer several advantages.

Some medium breeds are tougher, sturdier, and larger than smaller dogs, allowing them to handle vigorous activity better. If you try to jog with a small dog, you'll probably end up carrying them for the majority of the distance, but a dog like a cattle dog or collie mix would have no trouble keeping up.

Some of the medium dog breeds, such as the border collie, cattle dogs, German shepherd, and labrador retriever, are all used as working dogs because of their intelligence and eagerness to please. The medium-large and large dogs are quick learners and can learn a variety of tricks, and often have good behavior.

Medium dogs also take up less space and are easier to transport, and less expensive to feed and buy certain things for than large dogs. For many families, this happy medium makes for an ideal choice.

Medium-sized dog breeds are too numerous to list, and when mixed breeds are included, the possibilities are nearly limitless. Your local shelter has a large assortment in this size, and they may have a perfect fur baby waiting for you to find.

Medium dog breeds are frequently versatile and make wonderful apartment dogs, much like small dog breeds. They normally need more exercise than small dogs, but if you are prepared to take them on walks and find a spot where they can get some exercise by going for a run every so often, they are usually happy to live in the city.

Medium-sized dogs can live for 10-14 years on average, so they live long lives. However, you should research the average lifespan of any breed you are considering. If you love to travel, it's good to know that some hotels and motels will not accept dogs weighing more than 30 pounds, so plan ahead of time to ensure your accommodation.

Large Dog Considerations

A large dog weighs more than 55 pounds and can reach weights of more than 100 pounds. While all dogs, regardless of size or breed, can be trained, large dogs have been found to be more trainable and intelligent.

Big dog breeds are emotionally stable, well-mannered, and child-friendly than smaller breeds like chihuahuas (University of Arizona, 2019).

Large dogs can put up with rougher play and are truly gentle giants with big hearts. Living with a large breed dog in an establishment can be challenging to say the least. It can also be a unique experience, depending on the breed and size of your canine companion.

While some people consider a golden retriever or German shepherd to be 'large,' others compare large to a Russian wolfhound, great dane, or Neapolitan mastiff. Regardless of how you define 'large,' there are several factors to consider before purchasing a large dog.

The security factor is one of the most significant benefits of owning a large breed. Even if you don't feel the need for protection, and this is not one of your concerns.

Choosing a larger breed tends to frighten those who might be considering popping in for a visit. Large dogs are often clumsy and have big voices, and their "larger than life" physical presence often turns people off.

However, big dogs, contrary to popular belief, do not bark nearly as much as small dogs. Dogs frequently bark in response to circumstances such as alertness, nervousness, or attention. However, small breeds are more vocal in expressing their wants and needs. Although there is no such thing as a silent dog, you can rest assured that many large dog breeds prefer to remain silent.

Larger dogs are generally better suited for long outdoor excursions. If you enjoy hiking, camping, or other outdoor activities, they are always eager to accompany you, and possibly deter any wildlife from bothering you.

Bigger dogs require higher, sturdier, and more secure fencing. Every requirement will cost more because of its size. For instance, grooming, bed, bowl, jersey, dewormer, and the list goes on. They will also require a larger, more expensive crate, and you will need a larger vehicle to transport them.

Any fencing in areas where your dog will be permitted on your property should be at least five to six feet tall. This all depends on the size and weight of your canine companion.

Although all dogs shed fur, large dogs shed more than their smaller cousins. If you decide to bring a large dog into your home, you will quickly discover that your house will be dominated by your dog's coat.

If you allow your canine companions to use your furniture, you may need to buy more. A Russian wolfhound or St. Bernard will take up the entire loveseat, and most of the sofa in your living room will need to be cleaned every few months, with all the hair and slobber, etc.

One of the biggest disadvantages of a large dog is possibly its lifespan. Depending on the species, you could have them for as little as seven to eight years, whereas smaller breeds can live into their late teens. It's important to remember that every year you own a large dog should be cherished as there are fewer years to enjoy.

Purebred vs Mixed Breed

It is crucial that you consider whether you would prefer a purebred or a mixed breed and know of all of the factors that influence your decision. Perhaps you have fond memories of growing up with a particular breed, or you are looking for a dog with specific physical and behavioral characteristics.

Purebred Dogs

Purebred dogs, like all pets, have ups and downs in the breed. You can decide whether a purebred is a suitable fit for you, your house, and your lifestyle by being aware of the benefits and drawbacks of owning one.

Although a purebred dog may have desirable characteristics, some may also have health or behavioral issues. Dr. Greg Martinez, a veterinarian at Gilroy Veterinary Hospital in California and the author of *Dog Dish Diet*, said that all dogs are descended from the wolf, and current breeds occur only because people created them for specific purposes.

"By doing so, we risk a slew of hereditary issues," Dr. Martinez adds. As a result, it's critical to buy a purebred dog from a responsible and trustworthy breeder (Sundstrom, 2015).

In today's society, some people want purebred dogs simply because they are popular and have received media attention.

Dogs have become fashionable; however, when looking for the right pet, you must consider your personal preferences as opposed to those of the general populace.

The Art in Designer Breeding

Designer breeding is basically taking two different types of pure breeds and crossing them to create a new breed. Many of these designer dogs have taken years of trial and error to the point where breeders and the social market are satisfied. A first-generation, (F1-filial) generation, is a denoted generation.

For instance, the result is that an F1 goldendoodle is a direct and initial cross of two different breeds, implying that the parents are purebred golden retrievers and Poodles. The F1 Texas heeler is a direct cross between a blue heeler and a shepherd.

The F2 would be your second generation, and the progeny from this liter would be conceived from two of the first generations after mating. The two F2 hybrids mate and have a litter of pups, resulting in a third generation.

F1 and FB have significant differences (B-back cross). When the puppies are bred back to the parents, many traits differ due to the back crossbreed. There are a few differences between these two sets of genetic hybrids in terms of hypoallergenicity (the amount of shedding) and hybrid vigor. The more concerning aspect would be the potential health issues that could arise as a result of the interbreeding process (Seidl et al., 2019).

Physical Characteristics That Are Predictable

A purebred pet will usually have a set of physical characteristics as they typically all come from working dogs. As a result, when you adopt or purchase a purebred puppy, you will know the approximate size they will grow to be, as well as the type of fur they will have.

Temperament and Predictable Behavior

Pure-bred dogs have been bred for centuries to have specific temperaments. Poodles and Jack Russell terriers, for example, can be hyperactive, whereas basset hounds and pugs are much more docile. Knowing about these characteristics ahead of time allows you to make an informed decision about whether or not a particular breed is right for you.

Only purebred dogs are permitted to compete in dog shows sponsored by the American Kennel Club. As a result, if you want to compete in events like these, you should choose a purebred over a mixed breed. There are a few major cons when purchasing a purebred and I have stated them below:

Health Issues

First and foremost, a pure-bred animal has health issues because many breeders use inbreeding methods to preserve or enhance certain characteristics in a breed. Breeders have decided through the years which traits are desired for each breed through their development.

For instance, a cairn terrier became a small size dog, and border collies were designed and bred to be a medium size. Rottweilers have a short coat, while old English sheepdogs have a long coat. These desirable traits were bred into the gene pool by carrying traits from certain individuals. One of these individuals may be susceptible to a certain undetected weakness and this is also carried through to the breed because the gene pool has multiplied this particular set of genes for the best results in another area.

Unfortunately, this has made certain breeds more susceptible to specific diseases and illnesses. German shepherds, for example, are prone to hip dysplasia, whereas pugs and bulldogs frequently suffer from respiratory problems. Below are a few of the common problems coming through from purebreds.

Purebred dogs can have a variety of health issues:

- Disabling bone and joint conditions
- Eye diseases that cause vision loss or total blindness
- Heart diseases that drastically reduce a dog's life expectancy
- Diabetes and hypothyroidism
- Epilepsy and other seizure disorders

- Skin conditions that cause intense itching
- Chronic diarrhea and vomiting
- Kidney and liver problems
- Blood clotting disorders
- Cancer (this is the leading cause of death in a wide range of breeds)

If you buy a dog from a purebred dog breeder, the breeder will usually provide a health guarantee. Physical characteristics vary depending on the dog's parents, and personalities vary depending on who is raising them and in what environment they are raised. This includes other dogs, pets, or animals that share the area with them.

Some aspects of temperament, as well as behavior, are also passed down through the generations. If you need an energetic dog, select a breed that has high-energy genes. If you want a dog to herd your cattle, guard your sheep, hunt pheasants or rabbits, pull a sled, or do police work, you can select a breed that is prone to inheriting those behaviors.

Temperament and Behavior

Other aspects, such as temperament and behavior, are not inherited. Instead, they are primarily determined by the dog's surroundings, for instance, how he is raised and trained, starting from birth. Some dogs are influenced more by their genes, while others are influenced far more by their environment.

It is often more difficult to change a behavioral trait that has been 'hardwired' through a gene pool. To reduce conflict and stress, look for a breed with a temperament or behavior that is already close to what you can handle.

Working behaviors can be bothersome if all you want is a family companion and a pet. Most breeds were never intended to be 'just pets,' and trying to fit into a routine that you expect could just frustrate both you and the dog.

Certain animals are set in their ways, and they want to think for themselves rather than do what you want them to do. Working animals have a strong desire to do things rather than just hang around the house and yard. This can become a behavioral problem as they grow up.

They can also become suspicious or hostile toward strangers or start barking or howling into the night. All of these purebreds are meant to be predictable. The truth is that some purebred dogs do not "fit the mold" and are a throwback of their breed.

The next con is the expense when purchasing a purebred dog from a breeder. This can be much more expensive than adopting a mixed-breed dog from a shelter. Some purebreds can cost thousands of dollars, whereas adoption is only a few hundred dollars. If you insist on purebreds, you can try to adopt one from a breed-specific rescue organization.

To summarize, a purebred dog can be an excellent choice:

- If you know exactly what qualities you want in a dog
- If there is a breed that has all of the characteristics you desire. This is unlikely; compromise is almost always required when choosing a dog breed
- If you are willing to accept whatever other characteristics that breed has
- If you are willing to accept that there is an increased risk of health problems
- If you're willing to pay hundreds of dollars for a puppy versus adopting an adult dog from a shelter or rescue group that you were able to foster first
- If you get your puppy from someone who is doing everything possible to produce well-mannered, healthy puppies

Pros and Cons of Mixed Breeds

Mixed breeds were not intentionally bred and their parentage is frequently unknown. They are, however, very lovable dogs who often make excellent pets for people. Of course, there are benefits and drawbacks to living with any dog. If you are thinking about getting a mixed dog breed, here are some pros and cons to consider:

- Mixed dog breeds found at your local animal shelter can range from adorable young puppies to elderly dogs in need of a new home. It is estimated that 20 to 25 percent of dogs in shelters are bully breeds, also known as "pit bulls" or pit bull mixes, and, because of their bad reputation, these dogs can be difficult to adopt.

- Some cities and towns prohibit people from adopting pit bull mixes, which means they will be euthanized sooner or later. Most experts agree that these dogs do not deserve the bad press they have received and that if properly raised, they can make wonderful, loving pets.

Some people believe that mixed-breed dogs are healthier than purebred dogs. However, extensive health studies and actuarial records kept by dog insurance companies show that this is not the case. Surprisingly, large-scale studies show that mixed breeds and purebreds have virtually identical lifespans (Yordy et al., 2020).

The main disadvantage of mixed breeds is that they are less predictable than purebreds. It's difficult to predict how your mixed-breed dog will react to different situations. They might come from parents who have different behaviors and tendencies or because you may not know their parental history at all.

This makes it difficult to predict how they will act around small children and other dogs or pets in the household. You might not know how big the mixed breed will grow. These are a few things to consider when looking for a good match for you and your household.

Breed Temperaments

A Golden Retriever

A golden retriever is the epitome of a friendly dog. They are loyal, entertaining, and intelligent, and they adore everyone they meet. I think of them as beautiful animals that love to socialize all the time.

Labrador

A list of the best temperament dogs would be incomplete without mentioning the labrador retriever. The typical Lab is friendly and outgoing, eager to please its owner, rarely aggressive to people, and socializes well with animals. The darker labs have a lot of energy, which makes them ideal for active families.

The lab, like a bulldog, has an even temperament that makes them ideal for seniors. I find the tans are a lot lazier and tend to love their food too much. They all love water and whatever sport you will include them in. They just seem to be happy all the time!

Collies

Collies have wonderful reputations, and they, first and foremost, adore children and enjoy playing with them. They will adore you as well. This is because they thrive in the presence of all family members. While most collies may lack Lassie's abilities, they are gentle and affectionate, and these are qualities that make an excellent family dog. Don't be fooled by the size. These dogs can be gentle giants with training.

Saint Bernard

Saint Bernards will be patient and calm around children and are very protective of their loved ones. They are also large enough that small children will not injure them during playtime. They do, however, slobber but are fun to have around.

Great Danes

Great danes are large dogs as well. They tend to be a bit clumsy and come off as goofy, but they have a big heart for their size. Danes are affectionate and loving, and they get along well with other family pets. They are also highly protective of the people they care about.

Pug

The pug is at the other end of the size spectrum. These playful little pups were bred as companion dogs, and they generally live up to this description. Pugs will follow you from room to room, so get used to having a four-legged shadow.

Don't be fooled by the wrinkled face. These are alert little dogs that are tough as nails, and they are busy. They believe they should be running the show and have comical characteristics.

Boxers

Boxers are happy and fun, and it shows in their eagerness to play. They are also intelligent, so make sure they're properly trained from the start, or they'll outsmart you. These dogs adore their owners, and they need to be kept busy.

Boxers were nicknamed "the children's nursemaid" because they were originally from the United Kingdom and they are good with children. They are astute and tenacious but also brimming with energy and enthusiasm.

Stafford

Stafford enjoys being by your side while also protecting you and your family. The word "good-natured" perfectly describes this gentle dog. They adore children, are affectionate, and are devoted. They are also simple to train and are very human in their characteristics.

Their even temperament makes them suitable for people of all ages, including seniors looking for furry companionship. They love adventure and are extremely agile, but they can become obsessed with pieces of sticks and rocks at times.

TeaCup Poodles

These adorable fur balls enjoy your company no matter where you are. They might even follow you into the restroom. Another breed that adores children, they get along best with older children due to their small size. Teach your toddlers how to gently pet them. However, one advantage of their small size is that they are ideal for a good cuddle on your lap.

The Boston Terrier

These small dogs are friendly and enjoy being around people. In fact, receiving cuddles is clearly high on their priority list. They enjoy meeting new people and are always up for a game. They can be busy little dogs and love playing with the kids.

Irish Setter

The Irish setter is a friendly dog with a happy-go-lucky attitude who is a great giver of affection. These dogs have a lot of energy, but they are always up for a good time, and their love of exercise makes them excellent walking companions for both adults and children.

Cavalier King Charles

This little pup was also bred to be a companion dog, so it's no surprise that they enjoy social activities. These affectionate dogs enjoy being loved and are never happier than whenever they are snuggling up on the sofa with their owner.

These dogs get their sporty hunting nature from their spaniel ancestors. Nothing makes them happier than sitting on a lap, getting a belly rub, or sniffing out a rabbit.

Cockapoo

The cockapoo, a lively, outgoing dog, is one of the country's favorite dog breeds at present, and it's easy to see why. They are happy, eager to please, and enjoy being around humans. Play and cuddles are always at the top of their priority list!

These attractive little dogs have a disposition of a giant clown and may have been the first of the "designer dogs" (dogs that are not purebred), emerging in the 1960s rather than more recently.

Shih Tzus

Shih Tzus were initially kept by Tibetan monks and gifted to Chinese royalty. These tiny pups enjoy curling up on their owner's lap for a cuddle and thrive on their humans' affection and attention.

This little breed enjoys luxury and is exceedingly haughty and intelligent. It is a cheerful and adorable pet that likes to be around people. They love children and other animals and are affectionate, tough, and fiercely loyal. Hair must be regularly groomed to stay tidy and tangle-free.

Greyhounds

Greyhounds are fast runners and may give you the impression of having high energy, but they are actually amongst the laziest dogs out there. They typically have an even temperament, are kind, and get along well with both children and other canines. There is nothing they like more than watching a movie on the couch.

English Cocker Spaniel

This is a clever and controllable creature that is perfect as a family pet. An English cocker spaniel is an energetic dog who needs frequent exercise, and it is recognized for its attractiveness.

The right nutrition and exercise will help this dog live a long and healthy life. Their characteristics include being kind and affectionate, good with kids, intelligent, and cheerful.

Samoyed

The samoyed dog breed, originally bred to hunt, pull sleds, herd reindeer, and has proved to be a useful companion for the Samoyede people of northwest Siberia. Pack hiking, tracking, and warming their owners at night are among the responsibilities of the breed.

Samoyeds are a working breed. Thus, they occasionally have a strong will, but they are, above all, kind, gentle, and devoted family dogs. As long as new individuals don't mind minor shedding and stray hairs on their clothes, they are wonderful dogs to have.

West Highland Terriers

What a joy these cheerful westies are. They have a spring in their step and carry their tails high. They are well-balanced and have incredible adaptability designed in their character. They can easily just snuggle on the sofa and love their walks and outside activities.

Westies are petite, robust, and full of personality. These terriers are also quite intelligent and alert, but their independence can occasionally be a challenge when training.

Pembroke Welsh Corgi

This breed is a favorite of the Queen. Corgis are characters and make delightful companions. They love their humans deeply and are prepared to defend them with their bold and brave attitude.

A corgi is often joyful, intelligent, fun-loving, devoted, headstrong, and playful. You can't help but giggle when they are up to mischief as they are such cute little troublemakers. If they receive the right care and training, these dogs can make wonderful companions.

Cost of Care

The true cost of getting a dog goes beyond the dog's purchase price; long-term costs must also be considered. If you do a little research, you will discover that, while there are dozens of different types of dogs, some are more expensive than others. The purchase price of the dog, grooming expenses, and potential health care costs for the common breed are all factors that should be considered. Below are a few of the most expensive breeds to purchase and care for.

Yorkshire Terrier

Yorkshire Terriers, or yorkies for short, cost around $600 on average and have a life expectancy of 13 to 16 years. These tiny purse dogs are one of the most expensive dog breeds as they are prone to a variety of health conditions, including eye and knee issues, with potential health care costs. This dog can total $9,800. This high-maintenance breed doesn't shed much, but you should expect to pay around $31 per grooming session.

The Pharaoh Hound

The pharaoh hound, which is intelligent, active, and friendly, is one of the most expensive dogs, with an average purchase price of $1,250.

This large breed has an average life expectancy of 11 to 14 years and is generally healthy, with potential health issues costing around $1,500 to treat. Grooming costs for this short-haired breed average around $27.

The Ibizan Hound

The Ibizan hound is one of the most expensive dogs to own, with an average purchase price of $1,300. This dog breed has a life expectancy of 12 to 14 years, and both coat types; smooth and wire are easy to groom, costing about $25 on average.

Purebred Ibizan hounds have a low risk of hip dysplasia and a medium risk of deafness, with potential health care costs for general or common problems averaging $1,600.

King Charles Cavalier Spaniel

The Cavalier King Charles spaniel is one of the most expensive dog breeds to purchase due to its show dog status. The average purchase price for this dog is $1,250. However, grooming them is relatively simple, with an average cost of $55. This dog breed has a life expectancy of 9 to 14 years.

The Afghan Hound

The Afghan hound is a large dog that can be purchased from a breeder for around $1,000. These elegant dogs require daily hair combing due to their long, glamorous coats.

Professional grooming costs an average of $65 per trip, which contributes significantly to their status as one of the most expensive dogs. This breed has a life expectancy of 10 to 14 years and is predisposed to health conditions such as cataracts and hypothyroidism, which can come to $2,900 in health care costs.

The Lakeland Terrier

The Lakeland terrier, which was originally bred to hunt vermin in Northern England, is a smaller breed with an average price tag of $1,100. This is one of the most expensive dogs to own, as grooming will cost an average of $65, and finding a groomer familiar with this breed's distinctive style can be difficult.

A Lakeland terrier with a life expectancy of 12 to 16 years may also cost you around $1,000 in medical expenses.

St. Bernard

The calm and patient temperament will cost an average of $1,500 to buy. Grooming fees for this massive breed average $65, and its life expectancy ranges from 8 to 10 years.

Medical costs are the primary reason Saint Bernards are so expensive, with potential health care costs hovering around $8,600.

Old English Sheepdog

This dog is an excellent watchdog who gets along well with children. This is one of the most expensive dog breeds you could buy, with an average price tag of $1,250, standard grooming fees of $88 per visit, and potential health care costs of around $7,600. The average lifespan of this dog is 10 to 12 years.

The Golden Retriever

A purebred golden retriever, often described as the ideal family dog, will set you back around $1,500. Plan on spending about $56 each time you take this dog to the groomer.

This breed has an expected lifespan of 10 to 13 years, but they are inclined to have several serious medical conditions, including cancer, resulting in potential medical costs of $17,500, making it one of the most expensive dogs to add to the family.

The Irish Wolfhound

With an average price tag of $1,900, this gentle giant is one of the priciest canine breeds to buy and own. They are friendly animals and get along with everyone, but they also only have a lifespan of six to eight years. They cost around $65 to groom, and their potential medical expenses range from around $7,700.

Water Dog from Portugal

If at all possible, consider adopting a Portuguese water dog rather than purchasing one, which can cost up to $2,500.

This medium-sized dog enjoys the water, as the name implies, and each grooming session costs around $53. The breed's expected life span is 12 to 15 years, with potential medical costs of around $2,700.

Terrier de Russie Noire

With an average price of $2,000, black Russian terriers are one of the most expensive dog breeds money can buy. This large breed has a life expectancy of 10 to 11 years and expert grooming costs around $105. You should budget $6,000 for prospective healthcare to manage common orthopedic and eye problems.

Tibetan Mastiff

Finally, the Tibetan mastiff is the priciest dog breed to own. The average purchase price is $3,000. You may want to take advantage of the various tax breaks available to pet owners with this one.

Their life expectancy ranges from 10 to 12 years, and medical expenses can top $3,000 due to common health issues such as hip dysplasia, autoimmune thyroiditis, seizures, and more.

Family Considerations

Selecting the perfect dog for your family is a big decision. If you have a child, the possibilities are that you have a dog or will be asked to get one at some point. Having to care for a dog can help a child's self-esteem, ingrain a sense of responsibility, and help educate empathy for another creature. A family dog adores people, particularly children.

There is also no single breed that is ideal for the role of "family dog." Therefore, parents must first consider the disposition and personal characteristics of the individual dog. Below are a few main areas to look out for when choosing a pet:

- Your fur member should be outgoing and social
- Have a mild to a high energy level that blends in with the family
- Take pleasure in people, especially children
- Do not act aggressively around food, toys, or other valuable possessions

It is unreasonable to expect a child, irrespective of age, to be solely responsible for a dog's care. Dogs require not only basic necessities such as water, food, and shelter, but they also require consistent play, exercise, and training.

Teaching your pup house rules and assisting them in becoming a wonderful complement is too much for a young child to take on. While responsible teenagers could help with many tasks, they might not be willing to devote enough time to your dog. Please reconsider taking in a dog with the expectation that it will be the children's duty to care for it.

While your children are not the sole providers for your new dog, it is crucial that you all bond. Kids can connect with their new family members by going on walks and in teaching them tricks, and maintaining a feeding schedule.

It is an excellent opportunity for children to learn responsibility and for the dog to learn its place in the family. Just keep in mind that some dogs require more time to adjust and relate with the family than others. Below are a few ideas to consider when raising a pet:

- Diet, enrichment, sleep, caring facilities, and exercise
- Safety for your puppy
- House training
- Cleaning requirements
- Basic obedience
- Vet visit
- Dedicating enough time

Remarkable Dogs Stories

I have a wonderful story of a heroic dog called Swansea Jack who saved people from drowning.

A Story of Swansea Jack

A Flat-Coated retriever called Swansea Jack was small in stature, but what he lost in size, he made up in spirit. Swansea Jack lived in the North Dock with his master, William Thomas. When he heard cries for help, Jack would dive into the water and pull whoever was in trouble to safety at the dockside.

Jack's first rescue occurred in June 1931, a 12-year-old boy was drowning, and Jack pulled him out to safety. Jack rescued a swimmer from the docks just a few weeks later, in front of a crowd. His picture emerged in the local paper, and the city council presented him with a silver collar. His popularity grew, and eventually, the Star newspaper in London awarded him the prestigious "Bravest Dog of the Year" award in 1936 (Hembery, 2019).

Wrapping It Up

Main points to consider below are:
- Research the breed or look for behavior signs in a pet
- Work out a budget before acquiring a pet
- Ask yourself who will be responsible for the new member
- Have you all got enough time
- Is this the right time to bring a pet home
- How much space do you have

- Do you have enough time and patience for a puppy or should you adopt an adult dog

As you can see there is a lot to consider in choosing the right dog for your family and your household is definitely important, so, being as informed as much as possible before making this decision is vital to all involved.

Chapter 2:
Getting Ready for Puppy

"Happiness is a warm puppy." (Schulz, 2010)

When bringing a puppy home, you should be prepared for its arrival. Adding a new furry member to the house can be both exciting and exhausting. There is a lot of stuff you may want to collect for your newbie and a lot of it may be unnecessary.

With endless aisles of products, such as dog toys, dog treats, and dog foods from which to choose, pet stores can be overwhelming. To start, go through the food with your vet to make sure it's balanced and created especially for your developing dog.

I have set out an overall view of what is important so that you can make an informed decision. I have a formula and ideas to help you make up names too. There is a lot to cover, so, let's get started.

Tips on Choosing a Name for Your Puppy

What is in a name? Dogs cannot communicate, and we cannot tell whether the name is important to the human or the dog. Whatever the case may be, your new fur baby will need a name.

If you think about it, the majority of commands are one or two syllables long. This makes a word as simple as possible so that your pup will understand. The same reasoning can be applied to the name you give your dog. Any name that is longer than two syllables may be lost in translation from their ears to their brain (this is human reasoning).

Consider a name that starts with a sharp, distinct sound and ends in a vowel to make it ideal and as simple as possible to comprehend when they are called. For instance, a name that begins with the letters D, T, or K will be easy for your dog to remember.

A name that begins with the letter S or F, which has a softer beginning, can be more confusing for them. A dog's name should also end with a sharp 'A' or long 'e' sound. Again, this will be more distinct to their ears and easier to distinguish from other words.

Pick a good name that you adore as you will be using it frequently. Try out some of the names that you have chosen for your pup for a few days and see how they react to them.

You should also avoid any words that sound similar to a command or rhyme with it. For instance, if your dog's name is either Ray, Fay, or May, they can be confused with stay. It might also be difficult to get them to sit if you name them something like Kitt.

Make sure your pup's name is something you would be willing to shout out in public. Don't give your pup a name that others might find offensive or embarrassing. Try to avoid negative connotations and reflect on potential racial or cultural slurs, general insults, vulgar slang, and anything that contains a curse word.

The good news is that there are no hard and fast rules in determining which dog breeds should end in a vowel! This is because there are so many different meanings and sounds to choose from, any dog can have a name that fits within this theme.

If your dog is a pedigree, you could look into its heritage and choose a name from that area. For instance, you could call your German shepherd; Wolf Gang, Rommel, or Titus. You could also watch your fur baby and examine its characteristics. This could also give you an idea of what you would like to name them.

A dog that has distinct white feet and continually cleans, for instance, could be named 'socks.' A dog that is protective and likes to take over, if it's large and cheeky, you might consider 'Boss.' A small dog with a chip on the shoulder can be named 'Chip.'

'Chance' has a strong ring to it, but it can also convey a sense of vulnerability. An adopted rescue might receive such a name because everyone deserves a second chance. There could be some humor thrown into a name. For instance, a tiny tot could be named 'Bruiser' or a Great Dane could be called 'Tiny.'

You could name your newbie after important people or places. I know a person who named all his dogs after princes and kings. Allow your imagination to run wild and choose a name that everyone in the family will adore. Just end up making the name as simple as possible for your pup to remember. It could be one of the secret keys in establishing the best possible interaction for both you and your furry friend.

These suggestions are only ideas to help you to name your puppy. If brevity isn't your style and you want to give your dog a really long name, figure out the appropriate shortened version of the name, as this is what they will be called after a week or two.

Preparing for Puppy

I have listed a few supplies that you will need before bringing your new puppy home.

Food and Water Bowls

Dogs are notorious for spilling their food and water as well as tipping over their bowls, especially when they are puppies. Some even regard their feeding bowls as fun chew toys. Fortunately, there are numerous bowls available in various sizes, materials, and designs. Consider whether you will use a hand-me-down from other dogs.

It doesn't make sense to pay a fortune on bowls that your puppy will grow out of in a month. However, if your puppy will stay small and the bowl will suffice into adulthood, go ahead and buy a top-of-the-range-design.

Look for bowls that are simple to clean and will not tip over. Separate bowls for food and water are ideal and will minimize the mess factor. Of course, the puppy bowls you choose will be determined by your dog's portion requirements, and this will be based on its breed, size, and age.

There are many materials and types to choose from, such as stainless steel, elevated, ceramic, etc. Look for durability, dishwasher friendly, anti-spillage, heat resistance, and skid resistance bowls.

The slow feeder bowls are very popular. They can save your pet from a range of health problems and they are strong and will last as an heirloom.

Outward Hound provides options for big, small, and flat-faced dogs in four different styles and two sizes, something that no other brand provides. The non-slip base works well on all surfaces and prevents the bowls from moving while pets are eating.

Even the most ecstatic of our dogs managed to finish their meal without spilling or missing a bite. When compared to other slow-feed bowls on the market, the sturdy construction is especially obvious.

Puppy Feeding and Treats

There are certain times of day that are preferable to others for feeding puppies. You should feed your puppy immediately after your dog awakes in the morning (but after a potty break). Feed your puppy during lunch as you might be eating lunch at home or returning from work at this time.

Feed your puppy in the evening, ideally two to three hours before bedtime. This will give him enough time to digest the meal and relieve himself before turning in for the night.

Don't Feed Your Puppy Human Food

The digestive system of a dog differs from that of a human. A dog cannot properly digest typical human food because it is too rich and fatty; doing so can result in vomiting, diarrhea, and even more serious conditions like pancreatitis. Numerous human foods also have unhealthy levels of sodium for canines.

A mistake people make is that they underestimate a puppy and don't realize the heights it will strive to get food that has been left out. So, be conscientious of this fact and never leave food out as they are masterminds at finding food.

AAFCO Feeding Trials

You should buy puppy food from a company that has gone through AAFCO feeding trials. This includes the execution of diet formulations that have been tested and fed to dogs to ensure that there are no deficiencies.

Numerous pet food companies prepare their food according to a recipe and never test it on actual animals. The superior pet food companies are investing in science and consulting with veterinarian experts to provide food that's also perfectly balanced and free of harmful products that will be beneficial in your puppy's development.

Your puppy will need high-calorie food that is full of nutrition. This is because they burn up roughly half of their calories on tissue development and growth. The best puppy foods should be high in protein, calcium, and calories. A nutritious diet should be healthy, balanced, and high in quality food for a busy lifestyle.

A healthy diet will also lengthen a dog's life while decreasing the likelihood of disease. Consider that a Toy poodle puppy's bone growth differs greatly from that of a Great Dane puppy. This means that they must not be made to eat the same food.

Large breed puppy food contains specific calcium and phosphorus that are proportioned to ensure proper bone development, and this helps prevent joint disease in the later stages. The nervous system of a puppy is dependent on the essential fatty acid DHA.

Puppy diets should contain more of this essential fat than adult dog diets to help a growing puppy's eye, ear, and brain development. Puppies fed DHA-rich diets have improved memory and trainability, according to research. As a result, the puppies should be smarter and more trainable (Beynen, 2017).

Inter-Changing Foods

When changing puppies' food to another brand, you should start by mixing the new brand of dog food into the food they are accustomed to. This will give the puppy's digestive system enough time to get used to the new food.

Healthy Eating

Maintaining a healthy weight for your puppy is critical to his or her long-term health. Underweight puppies may not develop properly, whereas puppies that are overweight are more likely to become overweight adult dogs.

This can result in diseases such as arthritis, hypertension, cardiovascular disease, kidney disease from diabetes, and heat stroke. At each visit, your veterinarian should assess your puppy's body condition score to ensure that you are on track with nutrition.

When feeding a puppy for the first time, it's good to know that around 3 1/2 to 4 1/2 weeks of age, puppies should have started eating solid food. Make a gruel first by combining a milky-water with puppy food and let it soak. Serve it on a flat saucer.

Homemade Treats

Try your hand at making some popsicles with peanut butter. If your dog is feeling a little hot in the summer, this cool treat will certainly aid. You could add in apples; according to the AKC, apples can provide vitamin C, fiber, and calcium to your pet (AKC Staff, 2021).

You could also add in blueberries, carrots, sweet potatoes, and jerky. If you decide on commercial snacks, you should look for a superior branded company. Make certain not to over-treat when treating and remove a little of the food to compensate for the extra calories.

Dog Walking Gear and Protection

Collars

A martingale collar is my preferred collar for adult dogs. I say "for adult dogs" because they are slightly more expensive than standard flat collars, and puppies will often outgrow them. Simply get a flat collar for a puppy and then progress to a martingale when they are fully grown.

The genius of the martingale lies in its design. When the small loop is pulled, it partially closes the larger loop. This means that the collar closes tightly enough to keep the dog from slipping it, but not so tightly that it restricts airflow.

Make sure it fits properly when you put it on your dog. You should be able to get two fingers underneath it. Make sure that all your information and the name of your dog are on a dog tag, so they won't get lost because someone will know who to contact.

Leashes

Retractable leashes are not recommended because they constantly provide a sense of tension, which urges pulling. Even worse, larger dogs have the potential to break them. Choose a standard leash that clips onto a collar or harness instead.

Consider using a cotton training lead if you are going somewhere where your dog can have more freedom. These are longer varieties, and they range from 15 to 50 inchcs. You need control and obedience in a dog. 'To ensure this, your lead should be short between yourself and the dog. However, your ultimate goal is to get your fur baby to want to, not because it has to. So, let the lightweight lead loose on the ground.

Release the leash as the dog gets further away and reel it in as she or he gets closer. This way, if anything ever causes your dog to bolt, you can still keep control of them. Training leads can be worn over one shoulder and around the body like a side pack or wrapped around the waist to help free up your hands.

Harnesses

There are three basic harness configurations available. The back-clip harness is best for non-pulling dogs. When a dog reaches the end of the leash and you are using a back-clip harness, it will feel as though you are 'pulling' back. This will cause a natural reaction to pull away from whatever is pulling.

In this case, if your dog is a strong puller, a back-clip harness gives the dog leverage, which will encourage him to pull even more. If your dog has not yet been trained to pull on a leash, a front-clip harness is what you need. This harness will remove the dog's pulling leverage. When a dog begins to pull, the dog begins to rotate from around the clip, which causes the dog to turn toward you by replacing linear energy with rotational energy.

Teach your dog to walk on a leash. Your goal will be to transition your dog from a front-clip harness to a back-clip harness or just a collar. This brings me to a

Freedom Harness, which has both a front and back clip, and this is also my personal favorite.

Head Collars and Muzzles

I don't think head collars are necessary, a front-clip harness has always been plenty in my case. When you see a dog with a muzzle, there is a reason why it has one. Give these dogs plenty of room. You should not need a muzzle, but if you do for some reason I recommend the basket muzzle.

Protecting Your Dog If It Gets Lost

There is always the possibility that your dog will escape. If this occurs during your nighttime walks, you face additional challenges. As a result, you might want to consider some sort of visual marker. Reflective tape can be used on a regular collar or a reflective vest, or you can purchase a LED collar.

GPS tracker system

If you are interested in purchasing a GPS tracker system, 'Whistle' is a good one. The unit will cost around $150, and there is a monthly subscription fee of about $10 per dog. It also includes a health monitoring system.

Crates and Gates

Crates shouldn't be used as a form of punishment. Instead of confinement, regard a crate as a puppy's bedroom or private space. It provides a haven for a puppy to rest and relax, as well as a haven for your dog if you leave them at home or if a babysitter takes your place. A crate will prevent your puppy from roaming the house, discovering potential hazards, and getting into mischief.

Crates are commonly made of strong metal wires or sturdy plastic, and you will need to consider which material is best for you and your puppy. If you want to use a divider, you will usually find them on wire crates. It stands to reason that a metal crate will be more durable than a hardened plastic, but the metal ones also have better airflow.

Your crate should be large enough so that your dog can stand up, turn around, and lie down comfortably. It should be no bigger than that. Crate training is also useful for keeping puppies safe when you are unable to give them your full attention and should remain as a positive reinforcement.

Gates

Don't waste your money on a flimsy pet gate if you are trying to keep your dog out. You will need a strong gate that is made of a material such as tubular steel or textured graphite.

Gates like these are chew-proof and free of toxins that can harm pets and they expand from 29.5 to 38 inches, and this will fit most standard doorways. It has a handy walk-through door that can be opened and closed with one hand while keeping your dog where you want it. There are other options, such as sprawling room dividers and enclosed pens.

A bed

Although dogs are often content to relax their heads in a variety of places throughout your home, including your bed, it is critical that your fur-love has its own area for snoozing and sleeping at night. However, the selection of dog beds can seem limitless, making it difficult to choose one. Before you go shopping, consider your dog's requirements.

The breed, age, coat, size, and habits when looking for the best dog bed for your four-legged child. However, the most crucial factor is how your dog feels in the bed. Whether your pet genuinely wants to sleep there will depend on the materials, such as plush versus mesh.

Another area to look into is depth and height of the bed. With a firm, dense, memory foam mattress, the easy-to-enter orthopedic dog bed design should be cozy for older dogs who have aching muscles and stiff joints. For the head, legs, or anything else your dog chooses to rest on them, the cushioned bolster offers excellent support.

Bolsters have now been made tight and don't fall down, a problem with some other beds in the sofa style.

My suggestion is to first ask friends who are dog owners if they are happy with the dog bed they have bought. Often you will receive useful information. For instance: the material is not good, or the memory foam is of inferior quality, or it's not the quality they were expecting for the price they paid.

They might rave about the dog bed they bought a few years ago or know of someone that is happy with the outcome. All of these factors influence the best shapes, frameworks, and materials for your puppy to sleep soundly. Also, consider whether you require a waterproof outdoor dog bed or a comfortable indoor dog bed.

The designs are mind-boggling, with miniature sofas and bone pillows to match, canopy beds, chaise lounges, and dresser drawers. As you can see, they come in a variety of designs, including a slipper, a race car, donut, and hot dog bun. Tee-pees that are foldable or collapsible. Others can be used for camping, be inflated and deflated. Are you overwhelmed yet? If so, answer the questions below before buying a dog bed.

- Have you got a puppy or an adult dog?
- What size will your dog grow to, or how long are its legs and how big are its paws?
- Does your dog have health issues or is there a risk to health in the breed you have?
- Does your puppy rip everything apart or does your old dog have bowel incontinence?
- What is your climate like?
- Do your animals or family members suffer from allergies?
- Does your dog sleep huddled up or stretched out?
- What are you prepared to spend?

After answering all of these questions, you can put the rest of the puzzle together. You should be buying a bed that will last the lifetime of your dog unless your puppy tears everything apart. In that case, buy a cheap bed that you won't mind replacing.

Once you have established the size of your adult dog, add 8 t0 12 inches onto that length. If you have a puppy and you expect it to grow into a large size, you can use cushions and blankets inside a larger bed to make it cozy.

Memory foam does have an odor when it gets wet or absorbs sweat, so put a cover over it. Labrador breeds, for instance, often battle with aching joints as they get older. So, in saying that, a good orthopedic bed that has a high quality memory foam will suit them better.

Pee Pads, Grass Pad, or Litter Box

Laziness is not a valid reason to purchase an indoor doggy potty. Residing on the 17th floor or experiencing mobility issues that restrict you from carrying your puppy or taking your dog outside for bathroom breaks on a regular basis is. Doggy litter boxes and grassy pads are both popular and suitable indoor dog potty materials. Each has advantages and disadvantages. Other options are available as well.

Litter Boxes

Litter boxes are ideal for puppies because they provide clearly defined toilet areas and have raised sides that help prevent urine or bowel movement from getting on your floor.

Litter boxes come in a variety of sizes, so you can find something that is just right for your young pup. There are numerous liters to choose from, cat or dog litter will both work, and the majority provide some level of odor control.

Some homeowners clean a litter box every second day. You should, however, clean your box at least weekly. The disadvantages are that puppies can be reluctant to climb into a pile of litter, which may result in accidents. They might also decide to eat or toss the litter across the room.

Grass Pads

Grass pads help reinforce the relevant potty surface because they represent and replace the grass they believe they are relieving themselves on. Grass pads, such as litter boxes, provide a well-defined toilet area, and yet they don't provide much protection against mishaps or spillovers.

You could use a grass pad in a litter box. Although washable turf surfaces are generally easy to clean, many are difficult to remove from the pan without spilling waste. If you don't take care of your grass pads on a regular basis, they can become quite stinky.

Other Options

Pee pads or potty pads are absorbent pads that are usually used to line crates and protect your floors. They are, however, not without their flaws: The lining on the underside allows them to slide across surfaces and is easily shredded. They provide a well-defined target but do not have raised edges to help stop misses and spillover.

Pee pads are quite expensive, but manufacturers have developed odors to attract a puppy when it needs to use the restroom. They do, however, come in a range of prices, but you will be looking to purchase multiple absorbing layers, odor control, and the right fit.

Some animals simply don't like pads, so start with a small pack. There's also the old standby: newspaper piles. This is a low-cost option, but it can get messy if your puppy gets into it.

Toys

Provide toys with multiple functions, such as one to carry, one to care for, one to kill, and one to roll. Hide and seek, tug a war, and throw the ball are entertaining games for dogs.

Toys that have been 'found' are also far more appealing than toys that have been given. Making an exciting experience and an interactive game out of finding toys or treats is a good rainy-day activity because it uses up energy without requiring much space.

Many of your dog's toys should be interactive in some way. Interactive play is essential for your dog because they requires active and people time.

Your dog can release pent-up mental energy by focusing on a specific task, such as repeatedly returning a ball or playing hide-and-seek with treats or toys. All Dog Toys should be sized appropriately for your dog.

Balls, for example, must be big enough to carry but definitely not too small that they can be swallowed. Small balls and pieces that come off toys can quickly become lodged in the throat.

Puzzle Dog Toys

Puzzle dog toys are ideal for super-intelligent pets and canines who get bored easily. Treats are concealed inside partitions in puzzle toys, and your dog must figure out how they will get them.

Toys for dogs that are filled with pieces of dog Treats or, even better, a mixture of broken-up peanut butter snacks and jerky treats are such a delight for them. A puppy or dog can be entertained for hours with the right size dog treat toy. Your dog can only obtain the treats whilst chewing diligently, and only then are small bitesized pieces rewarded for their efforts.

Plush Toys

Plush toys with squeaking objects should be supervision toys if your dog feels compelled to find and destroy the source of the squeak. Several stuffing-free dog toys have recently been released, and these have quickly become fan favorites. Keep in mind that soft toys are not indestructible, but some are more durable than others.

Grooming Tools

Among the most essential at-home grooming tasks are brushing, bathing, and nail trimming. A short-haired dog will only need a rubber brush, and you can apply a dog moisturizer, to help the skin through a dry climate.

To gently remove eye boogers, use Angels' Eyes Wipes. They can also aid in the removal of porphyrins, which are iron-containing waste products excreted in tears and are the most common source of tear stain discoloration.

Electric dog clippers

Electric dog clippers get rid of stray entangled fluff. For dogs with an excessive fur issue that interferes with their toileting, just make sure not to point the blade at vulnerable places, and check regularly that they don't heat up and cause your dog any discomfort.

Blow Dryer

Allowing longer-haired dogs to air-dry causes mats and yeast infections. Use a fluffy towel to remove excess moisture before finishing with a blow dryer. Brushing the hair as it dries makes the process go faster.

Combs And Brushes

To start removing knots, gently separate the knot from the rest of the hair with a pin brush, then carefully untangle the mat with a sturdy comb. Starting at the top of the hair and working your way down toward the skin with a small flick of the comb.

Long-haired dogs that require frequent haircuts need a daily brushing to keep their fur mat-free. A slicker brush or more industrial brush is vital for a dog with a lot of undercoat, such as a German Shepherd or Golden Retriever. A slicker brush is preferable to the Furminator, which may overshed and strip the coat.

Pet Nail Clippers

When cutting nails, start by cutting just the tip off the nail. Trim it back a little bit at a time. Millers Forge Pet Nail Clippers are quite sharp and end up making clipping fast and painless.

Furthermore, their convenient grip makes them ideal to grasp. If you accidentally cut the quick of your puppy's nail, the powder can stop the bleeding quickly. Apply the styptic powder to a cotton ball and press it against the nail. If you don't have styptic powder, cornstarch or flour will work as a substitute.

Puppy Shampoo

Itchy skin will need a formula with oatmeal and aloe for puppies. Make sure to thoroughly rinse the coat and avoid getting shampoo in the eyes and ears. Even tearless shampoo can irritate certain puppies' eyes.

Puppy shampoos are typically gentler, with a no-tear formula, but still, try to avoid the eyes. Make sure to buy products with a good reputation and are a good household brand. I know of a case where a Great Dane died after being bathed with a store-bought shampoo.

If you bathe your dog too frequently, the skin of your puppy can become irritated as it continually strips away the natural oil from the skin. Some dogs, however, will require more baths, and this often depends on their breed, coat, and other factors, such as the area you live in.

Flea, Tick, and Worm Prevention

In addition to making your dog uncomfortable, fleas are the main cause of: Lyme disease, Ehrlichiosis, Rocky Mountain, Spotted Fever, Anaplasmosis, and tapeworm parasite whose larvae are carried by fleas, there are also other diseases that can be transmitted by ticks.

Comb through your dog's coat to check for fleas. Also, keep an eye out for "flea dirt," which are tiny black specks that are typically found on a dog's tummy or near its tail. Give your dog a tick check after going to wooded regions or spending a lot of time outside. This means looking for any embedded parasites. If you spot a tick on your pet, carefully remove the tick from your dog.

It is very important not to break the head of the tick off on the dog as this can lead to complications. Flea and tick products should not be used on puppies until they are at least seven or eight weeks old.

Once your fur baby is old enough, you must begin using a monthly flea and tick prevention medication to ensure that your dog is not bitten by fleas or ticks.

Many of the available treatments are effective against both fleas and ticks.

I highly suggest age-appropriate vaccinations, as well as Heartguard and flea and tick protection such as Frontline. If you walk your dog outside, which should be done frequently, you may not always see the dangers around you, but it's out there.

I know people who only use flea and tick medication during the summer. I prefer to keep it close at hand in case it is needed. My motto is prevention is better than the cure!

Puppy Proof Your House

There are many things that should be packed away or removed or changed before the puppy arrives.

Be Aware of Electrical Cords

Electrical cords from any equipment or appliance must not be left unattended. Puppies want to chew on them and can burn their mouths, damage gums, or even electrocute themselves and die.

Get a spiral cable wrap and encase your cords, this will keep them safe from curious puppies. PVC pipe and cord concealer will also work well. Make sure your cords are secure and cannot be accessed at all times.

Store Cleaners and Chemicals Out of Reach

Your home may pose some real dangers to your pet. Once a year the ASPCA's Animal Poison Control Center receives over 167,000 incidences of pet poisoning.

The good news is that by learning about these dangers, you can take the necessary precautions to protect your pet against it happening. Purchase proper storage or locks for your cleaning chemicals or use chemicals that are non-toxic.

Even the best pet-protection measures will fail if you do not insist on your family using something and then putting it back in the cabinet and locking it up properly. Cleaning chemicals should never be left unattended in your home because it only takes a minute for a curious pet to get its paws on them.

To prevent access to chemicals, use a baby lock. Most baby locks are also pet-proof, so locking the cabinet will prevent the pet from entering when you are not present. Never leave water or cleaning chemicals nearby.

Don't Fill buckets with cleaner and water or fill the sink with dangerous cleaning agents and leave the room, this will allow your pet access to the cleaner, increasing the likelihood that it drinks the cleaner or drowns in it.

Properly Store All Medications

Dogs are the most common culprits in FDA reports of pets accidentally eating medications, but cats and ferrets' curious-natured creatures can also get dogs into trouble.

Cats and sometimes ferrets push medication off counters, and a puppy will, of course, eat anything. Again, baby locks are best to lock up the medication with but you will have to get into the habit of putting it away again, else the baby locks won't help.

Your bags, purses, backpacks, gym bags, or diaper bags may contain one or more items that could endanger your new puppy. Xylitol poisoning is becoming more common as it is found in more products, such as sugar-free gum and some hand creams. So, keep bags behind closed doors or on a sturdy hook that is high and out of the way.

Keep the Toilet Lid Down

Puppies have already drowned in toilet bowls. Toilets are also unhygienic and poisonous with some of the harshest toilet cleaners, and you don't want your puppy drinking out of them.

To avoid this, make sure to close the toilet lid before exiting. If you are concerned that your puppy will be able to open the lid, consider purchasing a child safety latch to keep it closed at all times.

Keep Doors and Windows Shut

Remember to keep doors and windows shut and secure blind cords. This is especially important if you live higher than the first story because you don't want your pets falling out.

Keep Choking Hazards Away From Reach

Many people believe that giving cooked bones to their dogs is safe, but it is not. Cooked bones are extremely dangerous to dogs. Dogs can choke on whole bones or pieces of cooked bones that splinter. It's best to stick to chewing toys that are appropriate for your pet.

Gristle is a popular table scrap given to our dogs. Gristle is challenging to chew and has become one of the most common causes of a dog choking each year. So, instead of cooked meat and bones, serve some plain boiled chicken or vegetables if you want to treat them.

Secure Trash Cans

Dogs adore garbage! To a curious puppy's nose, trash cans are a mecca of exciting smells, so keep them covered and secured. A puppy can easily consume hazardous items or eat rotten things and cause bad bacteria.

If your trash can is not securely hidden in your kitchen cabinet, consider these three options:

- Human Butterfly Trash Can: The butterfly open top of this trash can, which is slick and durable, prevents your dog from poking his head inside. The silent close lid keeps your pup from becoming overly excited when he hears you toss food or rubbish out.
- Human Semi-Round Step Trash Can: A basic but excellent step-activated garbage can for humans with a sliding lock to keep your dog out of the trash.
- Rubbermaid Defenders Trash Can: With its steel outer shell, this trash can get most of its strength from its weight.

Move Poisonous Houseplants Out of Reach

Household plants liven up a room, but unfortunately, some species are toxic to pets and have been fatal when consumed. The plants on this list are toxic to your pet due to the toxicity they contain.

Many of these plants have different names, so it is recommended that all pet owners become acquainted with them. It's also a good idea to keep a first-aid kit on hand for your pet in case of an accident. Below I have a table with poisonous plants.

Table Of Poisonous Plants

Algaroba	Achira	Alyssum	Aluminum Plant	African Wonder

				Tree
Adam & Eve	Ambrosia Mexicana	Aloe	Alumroot	African Daisy
Acorn Squash	Amaryllis	Alsike Clover	Alocasia	African Violet

Cleaning Supplies

It's an issue not to have the necessary cleaning and deodorizing supplies on hand for a puppy's first 'accident' on the carpet. In addition, the new puppy's crate, food bowl, eating area, and toys must all be kept clean. Below I have cleaning supplies you will need to invest in.

Wipes

Disposable paper products are ideal for initial cleaning or picking up messes. Some wipes can be used on the pup directly if there are a bit still on them. For cleaning up messes on the floor, regular paper towels from the supermarket work just as well.

Soap

Antiseptic soap can be used to clean your hands before and after engaging in any "hands-on" activities with the puppy.

Disinfectant

Different disinfectants are effective against a variety of germs. Iodine-based products kill viruses and bacteria. Quaternary ammonium compounds may be helpful but are deemed inactive with hard water.

Odor Neutralizer

Liquids containing enzymes can break down molecules that are responsible for lingering live bacteria odors. Trace lingering odors from inappropriate urine or feces will attract a pup back to a previously soiled area as surely as a heat-seeking missile finds its heat source.

Some brands of cleaners, such as Odorban, Nature's Miracle, Odornil, Anti-Icky-Poo, and Nilodor, are natural, eco-friendly brands, and they work well.

Pooper Scooper

Pooper scoopers are used to keep the outside clean, and they assist in picking up the mess.

Latex Gloves

These may be useful when dealing with messy waste.

Carpet Cleaner

Try and look for enviro-friendly products such as these below:

- Salsus, which is biodegradable
- White house natural cleaning
- Bonami

Poop Bags

Small disposal bags are used to keep solid waste deposits contained.

General Cleaning Supplies

These are supplies such as buckets, mops, brooms, trash bags, and laundry detergent are required for washing puppy blankets and soft toys.

Remarkable Dogs Stories

A Story About Glenn and Buzz

A Jack Russell terrier named Glenn is completely blind and dependent on his best friend Buzz, a Staffordshire bull terrier. This inseparable team has a wonderful relationship that extends to compassion and beams of love.

Glenn's lead is connected to Buss' collar, and he follows Buzz wherever he goes. Often you will see Buzz assisting his blind friend at the shelter to find his bed, food bowl, and kennel by gently nudging him when he strays. The two were discovered inside a sea tunnel in the North of England and have remained inseparable since; once separated, they become restless and agitated.

They are now being cared for at the Stray Aid rescue center in Coxhoe, Durham, not too far from where they were discovered in Hartlepool. The staff has no information about the dogs' background, but they believe they are about 9 or 10 years old (Toussaint, 2015).

Wrapping It Up

- When naming a dog, it should be two syllable long, starting with a distinct sound and ends in a vowel
- Purchase interactive toys for puppy but check for safety as it is a priority

- Slow feeders prevent several health issues from occuring
- The correct dog food can extend your animals life
- Back-clip harness gives a dog leverage to pull but a front clip harness removes that option
- Never leave a puppy unoccupied-other options are gates or a cage
- When looking for a bed, size and health issues need to be addressed
- Puppy pee pads, grass mats, litter boxes can assist in potty training your fur baby
- You can do your own grooming at home and, in this way, you can avoid harmful parasites
- Puppies are no different to a baby and a house needs to be puppy proofed
- Use baby locks on chemical and medicine cabinets
- There are dangers inside a house as well as outside-poisonous plant
- Try to use eco-friendly natural cleaning products, it's safer

Now that we have covered all of that, you are fully prepared for your puppy's arrival. How exciting it is to bring him or her home!

Chapter 3:
The First 24 Hours

"No matter how you're feeling, a little dog gonna love you."
(Waka Flocka Flame, 2020)

It's finally time to welcome your new furry child into its new home. If you have taken all the necessary precautions to puppy-proof your home before their arrival, it is going to be a joyous occasion.

Have a quick look around to see if everything has been removed that could potentially harm your fur bundle. This will include removing medicines, chemicals, handbags, and plants that are toxic to dogs.

Choose a room for your furry child to settle into for the first 24 hours. A frequently used room with easy-to-clean floors will be ideal! This simply means that your pup will not feel isolated and will be able to explore small areas of the house first. If your room is large and there are areas you are concerned about, this will be a good time to use your sprawling room dividers and make the fur pups area smaller.

Steps to a Good First Day and Night

Before you introduce your pup, make a list of puppy house rules and clarify them with your family. Each member must be consistent and on board with the puppy training. A puppy will become easily confused if one family member doesn't allow them on the furniture, but another encourages them up.

Furthermore, if left unchecked and to their own devices, new puppies will quickly develop very cheeky habits. If you allow them to beg at the table and expect that the dogs won't bother you at every meal, you are in for a surprise!

There are also some ground rules to establish with the human members of the family. If you have a puppy that enjoys chewing things, for example, leaving an expensive pair of sneakers within their reach is a recipe for disaster.

It's necessary to keep in mind that your new puppy has just been separated from everything it ever knew-its siblings and mother, and it might be nervous in the new environment. It may take time for them to adjust to their new surroundings and smells.

Introducing Your Puppy

Make the welcome party as small as possible at first; this can only help their possible nerves. Too many new places, smells, and people may simply confuse and scare them. Allow them to explore a designated area instead, perhaps where it gets their food and water.

They need to be acquainted with the small, puppy-proofed area where you have placed their bed or crate. To begin, keep other pets in different areas of the house; after all, it can all be a bit too much. Let them explore at their own pace, while always keeping an eye on them to make sure they don't get themselves into any trouble!

Speak Calmly

Speak calmly and make sure your family members keep their excitement in check and use a calm tone to create a peaceful and non-threatening environment, which will help your puppy feel more at ease.

Don't give your puppy food as a reward for interacting with new people. Some dogs will continue to take food even when they are afraid, so even though they are making contact, the overall experience is detrimental to their emotional well-being.

Don't rush the process, give the puppy plenty of time to get to know each new person. If they have a positive experience throughout these introductions, it will help them when they meet and socialize with new people outside of the home.

Watch Your Puppy's Body Language

It is critical to be aware of your pet's body language. Do not chase your puppy around, and grab it or hold them if they want to be released. You want your fur child to begin their life with you in the same way that you want them to end it: trusting you, trusting your hands, and trusting everyone in the family. Sit on the floor with them and let them set the pace of your interaction.

Spend as Much Time With Your Puppy as Possible

Make sure you have time to devote to your new arrival to help them adjust to their new surroundings and establish a routine. Working from home or taking a few days off will enable you to spend quality time and bond. Puppies need to learn about their new world; what people are like and who to trust during their first few weeks of life. Make certain that you are present to guide and help them through every step.

Put a plan in action to avoid having to return to work unexpectedly. Don't just leave for work and come back to chewed-up furniture and meet up with an anxious, panicked pet. Make sure they are only left at home for short bursts of time and steadily increase the periods.

Make Your Puppy Feel at Home

It doesn't take long to make a puppy feel at home and at ease in its new environment. By stepping back from the excitement of introducing the new puppy, and remembering that their entire world has changed and everything is new to them, you will want to make their homecoming a fun and wonderful event.

All you have to do now is take the opportunity to get to know your fur baby, and for it to bond with you, this can be done through playing, training, socializing, having fun, and watching your puppy grow.

Show Them Their Sleep Spot

Your new puppy is still growing, and it is possible that they will fall asleep in the most unexpected places, including during playtime. Puppies sleep between 15 and 20 hours per day, and while they frequently stop in their tracks and fall asleep, it is crucial that you don't disturb their sleep. The sleep on the floor is likely just a quick power nap before returning to play, but they need their sleep at this young age, especially with all the excitement of a new home!

The first night may be difficult for both you and your pet. It's their first night away from their mother, which is bound to be a shock. This means you might have a rough night ahead of you, however, there are a few components you can set up that will help them settle down before bedtime.

Let Your Puppy Identify With Something Familiar

Place an item of clothing, such as a t-shirt, with your scent or the environment next to them while they sleep. This will help them identify with something familiar and ease into their new home transition. You can also hide a toy with a scent for your puppy to find in its cordoned-off area.

When stimulated mentally and physically, it causes the puppy to become aroused, tired, and ready to sleep. So, tossing a toy, playing hide-and-seek, or experimenting with name recognition by forming a circle and taking turns calling your new addition.

Rewarding your fur child with dog treats when it's busy playing can also be an ice-breaker. As your pup begins to slow down and look tired, play classical or soothing music to lull it before bedtime. This should help reduce the whining and anxiety while the drowsiness sets in and the other noises or unfamiliar sounds become quiet.

Regardless of how simple it might sound, to sleep with your fur baby will not set a good precedent. Believe it or not, it will make for an easier second night if you let your pup have its own space.

Introduce Rules Right Away

Although it may appear premature to you, your pup needs to learn the house rules from the start. Its day will be better adjusted and happier if it is more structured and consistent.

Use gentle redirection to discourage chewing or any other undesirable behavior. Yelling or punishing them will only frighten and confuse them, and you won't teach them anything. Remember that they are still learning what is expected of them. Praising them for good behavior and deflecting unacceptable behavior is an effective method of assisting their learning.

Gradually build their environment by adding to it, under your supervision. They learn quickly where their new place is in the 'pack.' Give them lots of affection and a lot of love, consistent rules, and routine. Keep rewarding good behavior and gently correct unacceptable behaviors. As they adjust to their new surroundings, you will form a bond with them that will last their entire life.

Take Things Slowly

Don't expect your puppy to walk confidently and playfully through the door. They may, but they are far more likely to be tentative, wary, and uncertain as they try to figure out what the next stage of their lives will bring.

Their new life may appear strange, unfamiliar, and potentially frightening. You know your fur child has 'come home,' that you will love and keep happy and healthy, but your puppy doesn't know that yet. Be patient, and your pup/dog will adapt quickly.

Keep pup's arrival as low-key as possible, no matter how excited everyone is. It's so simple to lavish affection on the new fur bundle. Always oversee excited children and give your fur child some much-needed moments away from the excitement, while it's getting accustomed to the surroundings.

Set an Alarm

Set an alarm to take the puppy out every few hours. Again, introduce rules right away, and this includes housebreaking rules. Until your puppy becomes potty trained, it will most probably wake you up to go outside. Lining your puppy's crate or area with a pee pad is a good idea.

Most dogs do not like to mess in their sitting or sleeping area. If their crate is close to you, they will most likely wake you up. If their crates are too big, they will probably soil a corner. If you or your puppy sleeps well, you may want to set an alarm to prevent accidents in the crate or bed area they are sleeping in.

Midnight Potty Call

When you get up to take your fur baby out at midnight, try to remain as neutral and as quiet as possible. Don't let them think it's playtime, be gentle and try not to interact with them. However, puppies and children usually wake up around 5:30 a.m.

You might just have to adapt and embrace the mornings with a busy puppy. Allow them to go outside for a potty, and if you tend to sleep in, bring them back into their sleep area and place a chew toy with them. They might play a little and fall asleep again for a while. But once they are awake and alive-wire, take them outside again for a potty and feed them, play with them for a few minutes and carry on to follow their schedule.

Remarkable Dogs Stories

A Story About Barry, a St Bernard Rescue Dog

Barry der Menschenretter was born in 1800 and passed away in 1814. This St. Bernard worked as a mountain rescue dog for the Great St Bernard Hospice in Switzerland and Italy. He existed before the appearance of the modern St. Bernard and looked a lot smaller in stature.

Barry was dubbed "the most famous St. Bernard" as he was credited with rescuing over 40 lives throughout his lifetime. Hence his byname Menschenretter, which means "people rescuer" in German.

The legend states that he was killed while busy with a rescue, but this is not true. Barry retired to Bern, Switzerland, and his body was given to the Natural History Museum (Wikipedia Staff, 2021).

Wrapping It Up

- Be prepared, communicate puppy rules to the members of the household
- Sort out a room that the puppy can be kept in for 24 hours
- Gradually introduce the family as the puppy can get overwhelmed

- Busy puppy with games before bedtime and afterward, play soothing music
- Introduce puppy house rules immediately
- Take things slow
- Set alarms for potty visits at night

If you prepare ahead of time and have covered all the areas and set up for your puppy, the transition should be relatively easy. Remember to go at the puppy's pace and be patient.

Chapter 4:
Potty Training

"Dog training is a never-ending process of evolving." (Balabanov, 2022)

The benefits in a potty training with a schedule, is that it gives a plan of action for new puppy parents to follow. As you can see below, small puppies need to use the toilet often. However, there is a problem with the schedule too, as there is always an exception to the rule and some puppies can't wait till it's their designated pee time.

So, what I'm saying is, don't be a slave to routine! It's normal to have the occasional potty accidents in the house during training. The key is patience, consistency, and a whole lot of praise, and you will achieve your goal.

The foundation for your relationship with your new fur member must be built in trust and love. To teach your pup good potty habits. I have set out two potty-puppy schedules below. One for puppies that are eight weeks old and another from 3 to 4 months old puppies.

Create a House Training Schedule

The 8-Week Puppy Potty Schedule

2 am	Night shift; some puppies require the potty at night for the first few days, while others require it for a week or two, and then there's the exception.
6 am	Unfortunately, there is no snoozing in for puppy parents. The first potty of the day is crucial!
7 am	This is normally 10 minutes after breakfast
9 am	Mid-morning
11 am	Potty often occurs after the second meal of the day
1 am	Remember to always take the puppy outside when he wakes up from a nap
3 pm	This potty occurs after the third meal of the day
5 pm	Puppies often get excited at this time-another important time to go pee!
7 pm	This potty break occurs after supper, the final meal of the day
11 pm	If your puppy is sleeping-you can skip this time slot

The 3 to 4 Months Puppy-Potty Schedule

6 am	The first potty of the day is still an urgent one!
9 am	Mid-morning
12 pm	Often after (second meal of the day)
3 pm	Mid-afternoon
6 pm	Often after supper (final meal of the day)
9 pm	Older puppies are more alert in the evenings now
11 pm	The last trip outside before bed

What Does Your Pups "Bathroom Success" Sound Like

Praise your fur baby with enthusiasm, 'Yay!' Puppies often respond by wagging their tail and a happy sway of the butt to that 'Yay' remark! Make sure potty training is a positive experience.

This is the best time to reward a puppy after a successful potty in the right place. Don't be shy, dance, show your happiness. Clap your hands, sing your pup a song, whatever works but make the experience positive. Love and cuddle them as you give them a delicious treat, positive reinforcement for a good job, well done.

Keep an Eye on Puppy

If your home is extensive and you are constantly running around trying to find and watch out for your fur baby, it's time to confine your pup in a smaller area. Another option is to let your pup have a 'time-out' in the crate.

Keep an eye on your puppy at all times, particularly when they go outside to relieve themselves. Take puppies outside with the aid of a leash, so you won't lose them.

Use the same command every time, such as "go pee" or "go potty," to encourage your puppy to relieve itself. When you keep going to your puppy's favorite place, they will eventually follow you instinctively and understand the instructions.

Control Feeding

Don't "free feed," free feeding comes with several issues. First off, because your dog eats and drinks all day long, you cannot keep an eye on their 'intake' and 'output.'

Due to the uncertainty surrounding its eating habits, you can't follow a schedule, and you don't know when to take your pup outside for potty training. This becomes extremely challenging, to say the least.

Another big problem is that you may not immediately notice if your dog stops eating due to illness. This could be dangerous, as you might have no idea how sick they are until it's too late.

Additionally, it will be challenging to keep food available at all times if you ever intend to travel with your pet. You would normally need to feed your pup a few moments before you come to a stop, so they can relieve themselves.

How to Feed Your Pup

Whatever isn't consumed during 15 minutes of placing the food down must be picked up. Puppy love will eventually learn to eat faster when the food is placed down in front of it.

A spoonful of wet food mixed with a little hot water over their pellets works well if they are picky eaters. However, keep in mind that wet dog food can stain teeth and necessitate more dental visits than normal.

Feed your pets at consistent times each day. What goes in usually has to come out within 15 to 30 minutes. As a result, after feeding your pet, wait 15 minutes unless you see the warning signs (that puppy needs to go potty) and take them outside immediately for a bathroom break. This would entail limiting your dog's mobility to being tethered to you, in a crate, or a puppy-proofed area.

Praise

Wait to praise the puppy until it's done with its potty, so you don't distract it from what it's busy doing. Love and praise your fur baby, never undervalue the influence of touch and loving your fur baby.

Your pet will know from this affection that you love them and you are happy with their successful effort. A good, hearty rub behind the ears or on the belly is a reward.

Did you know your fur pup loves spending special time with you even more than treats and belly rubs? If everything goes well and the puppies' toilet is successful, take your little one on a special walk. You could take them to a dog park for some bonding time where you can play fetch, throw a Frisbee, go for a run, or just enjoy the walk.

This special time you spend with them will not only show them that you are proud of them. It will enable a unique bond to emerge and this is to be cherished.

Use Their Crate in Training

When training puppies to potty while using a crate, pay attention to their schedule and place them in their crate 15 to 20 minutes before potty time. Take them out to the potty once they have done their deed successfully and in the designated potty location, reward and praise them.

Leave them out of their crate until it's almost time for their next trip to the potty. If they don't need the potty, place them back in the crate for 5 to 15 minutes (the time will depend on the size of the puppy) and try again.

The size of your dog's crate shouldn't be too large. If it's too big, your puppy might think they can relieve themselves in a corner while still maintaining a tidy 'home,' and this would defeat the goal. To keep your fur child feeling connected rather than alone, place the crate in a high-traffic area within your home.

A portable crate that you can move from one room to another is another option. Concerning feeding decisions, you should feed your fur bundle a routined schedule as this will make their potty predictable. You will often notice a pattern emerging, and once you do, you will predict the next bathroom intervals.

The Do's and Don'ts

Physical punishment is no longer regarded as correct and against the law in some areas. Instead of using painful punishment, puppy trainers use more socially acceptable deterrents like jabbing or prodding the dog with a finger or correcting it with an alpha roll. However, the effectiveness of these techniques in curtailing bad behavior is still up for debate.

One of the main dangers of hitting or beating a dog is that it might come to believe that we (and all other people) are untrustworthy and cause suffering. Because of this, it is crucial to change the direction of our aversive approach.

Pets might associate a hand or a person approaching as a threat if we spend the majority of our time physically slapping them. There could be some serious reactions to this type of discipline. Below are a few behavioral signs:

- A more self-assured and combative dog will likely strike back to dissuade the threat.

- Less dominant dogs may opt for pacifying behavior in that they will submit and roll over and show their belly.
- Other submitting behaviors: lip-licking and turning away, showing you it wants to avoid conflict by demonstrating capitulating behavior-they are not a threat.
- You may also have a dog that will cower and urinate at the harshness in your voice.

Lack of trust, as well as increased anxiety and stress, will leave you with an unpredictable animal, so don't hit your puppy.

Don't Rub His or Her Nose in It

Rubbing a puppy's nose in their potty is unhygienic. If your dog is in good health, this behavior won't make them sick, but it's not pleasant. Dogs consume their own waste regularly, and the worst disease they could contract is an extension of the life cycle of worms that they already have inside their bodies.

Dogs are not as bothered by the smell of their feces and urine as we are. Wastes play a crucial role in how dogs interact with other members of their species. In saying this, there is no reason you should rub a puppy's nose in their potty. It serves no purpose.

Signs That Your Puppy Needs to Relieve Itself

When some puppies need to go potty or urinate, they are quite frank about it, but some are subtle. In general, it is simpler to spot warning signs in older puppies. Young puppies can't communicate their need to go potty in a timely manner. Below are a few signs to look out for.

- Sudden changes in play, conduct, or activity
- Patrolling, circling
- Whining
- Advancing toward the door; pawing or scratching at the door
- Returning to a once dirty spot in the house
- Puppy smelling or licking its rear or groin area

Remain Calm

Finding your puppy's 'accident' in the middle of the floor when you walk into a room is not a particularly pleasant experience. This is especially true for new puppy parents. And let's face it, we frequently react by losing our temper and becoming angry.

However, this will achieve nothing good, so stay calm and cool-headed when handling the situation inside your house. While you should be aware that accidents are a normal part of the house-training process.

Once you see the warning signs, immediately direct them outside to their designated potty spot. Keep trying this method, be consistent, even with a few failed attempts, be patient, and don't ignore the situation either!

Firmly Say 'NO'

When finding a puppy potty inside, immediately fetch your puppy and take them to the scene of the crime. Give him or her a chance to smell the area before firmly objecting by firmly saying 'no.'

Take the paper towel and its contents outside with them, to the location that you designated to be a potty spot, and lay it on the ground. Allow the pup to once again smell the contents. This is when you say, "Go Potty."

Clean the Mess up Quickly

Clean up the mess as quickly and effectively as possible. The idea is to gather any remaining mess or soak up any urine with a puppy pee pad, coffee filter, or paper towel and throw it away once used.

Next, use warm water to sponge the area (ring the sponge of excess water). Put some natural cleaner or digester on the area, leave for a minute and sponge it out with the warm water again.

There are some excellent inexpensive wet vac options, but the Bissell Cross Wave is highly regarded and praised by many pet owners.

The damp area will receive a final coating of baking soda. Baking soda absorbs any leftover moisture and guarantees that no stain or odor is left behind. Once the area has dried, vacuum it up.

Bell on the Door

There are a few different methods you can use to allow your dog to express the need to go outside. The simplest and least expensive solution is to hang bells from the doorknob or close to the door.

Additionally, you can install receivers all over your house, and in this way, you will hear your pet ringing the doorbell from all the different rooms. The most technologically advanced choices are talking buttons and recordable buttons. In using the latest technology, people are teaching their pets to communicate.

Stopping Future Accidents

When stopping further accidents, say something similar to 'Eh-eh' or 'Whoops.' This should stop the puppy from urinating. Another efficient way to stall them is with a sudden noise that causes them to stop in their tracks (but don't make the noise too loud).

In each of these situations, take them outside right away so they can finish urinating before rewarding them with a dog treat. You want your new puppy to learn that going outside to relieve itself constitutes a positive reaction.

Take Puppy Outside More Often

If your puppy is still messing, even though you are keeping to the schedule, you should take them out more frequently. Start them off by taking them out every 30 minutes.

Take your pup outside to a specific location and instruct them to "go potty." Your puppy will go potty more frequently in the grass. If you take them regularly, this will hasten the process of housebreaking.

Potty Training in an Apartment

When you live in an apartment building, potty training your puppy is a completely different game. When you see a warning sign, you can't just pick up your puppy and run out the back door into the yard. Even though you live in an apartment, you can still successfully train your dog to 'go' in the proper locations.

Start by feeding your puppy or dog a scheduled meal, as I have explained. Follow by taking your pet to a designated area that you have created and giving the command. After the puppy does its potty, leave it to play for about 45 minutes. Leaving your fur baby to play will aid in getting all its energy out before taking it back to its crate. Wait 15 minutes before it's time to take the puppy back to its potty area.

Proceed with this pattern till the next feed with hourly intervals in between the last potty. You may be thinking to yourself, 'wow,' your precious bundle of fur seems like a little potty machine. Your pup might need to go tinkle often, but your situation will improve when your pup gets older and has more control of its bladder and bowels.

Additionally, young puppies should eat, drink, and play within five to ten minutes of waking up and emerging from their crate. The most popular choice when creating a potty area is using real grass blocks of lawn.

Fresh pieces of lawn are delivered to apartments in the city every month. The other option is artificial grass on top of the litter. This is a convenient alternative to having to wait for an elevator. Your replacement 'garden' can be kept inside the house or outside on a balcony.

If you are using a porch toilet or potty pads, you will need a convenient place to dispose of any waste. Invest in a small dog waste station with a deodorizer, such as the one PetFusion has. This will stop you from having to make a trip to the trash every time your puppy poops.

This product is lightweight and portable, and it comes with a locking lid and a charcoal filter that helps to reduce the odor. These features make trips to the complex's garbage less frequent; it's convenient.

Remarkable Dogs Stories

Dozer Supports Cancer Research by Running the Marathon

The Maryland Half Marathon benefits the University of Maryland's Greenebaum Cancer Center. Dozer, a goldendoodle, seems to act like any other normal dog. He loves to play catch and go to the beach, and he really loves people.

But he's actually been busy with doing what other humans usually do—drumming up support for Cancer patients. Dozer attracted the attention of more than 2,000 runners after breaking free of his invisible fence and joining the marathon. He started approximately five miles into the race, from a little place called Howard County, Maryland.

He crossed the finish line at 2:14 and came in 24th place. Jon Sevel, a co-founder of the Maryland Half Marathon, claimed that many participants saw Dozer at various points on the course, drinking from cups at water stations. Nobody realized the dog was actually running his own race.

After finishing the last seven miles, Dozer found his own way home on Monday morning. After his owner took him for a precautionary vet check, Dozer was given a bill of good health and was awarded a medal by the race directors.

Karen Warmkessel, the spokeswoman of the University of Maryland Medical Center said, "*This is a very sweet dog. When I saw him today, he looked great. He was really active, and now he's raising money for cancer research*" (Neumann, 2022).

Wrapping It Up

- Try and keep to a potty schedule
- The schedule will change as the puppy gets older
- Don't hit your puppy
- Keep an eye on the puppy, especially when they are outside
- Don't overfeed your puppy
- Be patient and always praise

As a pet owner, your goal should be to raise a confident and content dog by giving them lots of praise and frequent potty breaks. In doing this, it's important to note that your puppy still needs your patience and love while potty training. Regular house-training schedules are necessary to successfully house-train a puppy.

Housebreaking a puppy is similar to potty training a child and the earlier you start training and being constant the better. Additionally, giving the puppy the attention they need will result in a happy, trained puppy.

Spending time with the puppy early on in its life will save you time, effort, and frustration in the long run.

Chapter 5:
Other Essential Training

"It's easier to steer than to stop a dog." (Mackin, 2022)

Crate Training

Your dog isn't 'imprisoned' during crate training. It offers them their own space and helps soothe anxiousness. By using treats and activities, you may help your pet develop a pleasant association with the crate. Be patient; crate training may require six months of regular practice.

Pick the Right Crate

There are a few things to think about when selecting a permanent crate solution for your home. You might want to choose a sturdy container or one that goes with your decor in the area you are placing it.

Soft-sided pet carriers are a good option for traveling, to the beach, or to the veterinarian. The American Veterinary Medical Association recommends that travel carriers should be big enough for your dog to stand up, turn around, and lie down in. They also recommend that crates have ample ventilation on both sides of the crate.

Leave Your Scent on Clothing in a Crate

As I have stated before, the scent of a person or their surroundings is important when putting a puppy at ease. So don't forget to put a T-shirt or scarf with your scent in the crate. When beginning crate training, open the crate door and give a command for the puppy to enter the crate.

Give your pet a voice cue, like 'crate,' to enter. Pointing towards the interior of the crate while holding a treat will entice them. Puppies should be glad to enter if you have placed a small food treat inside as well, but position the treat towards the center of the crate and wait.

Leave a Treat in the Crate

When your fur child goes to retrieve the treat, praise your puppy and let it investigate the contents of the crate, it may move in and out and play around it. Keep the door of the crate open and carry on to repeat the process until your puppy eagerly enters the crate.

Once the puppy is comfortable with its surroundings and starts to sleep in the crate, repeat your actions, but this time place the food treat at the back of the crate.

Encourage the puppy to go into the crate on their own once they are tired so they can have their treat and chew on a toy before nodding off into a dream world.

You can now gently close the gate but stay close to the crate to calm the puppy if it wakes and feels confined. If crates are used correctly, a lot of destructive activities, such as chewing on a table leg or just becoming destructive, can be avoided.

Never Crate After Punishing

Never crate after correcting your puppy for inappropriate behavior. The crate will stand out negatively, and associations will be made towards a disdainful emotion in regard to a crate. A pet owner's attitude should be praised and a big deal made when a puppy goes into a crate and stays there and when puppies leave the cage, the owner should treat this as trivial.

Don't Treat Bad Behavior

Don't ignore the behavior of a bark or whimper by giving puppy treats, and never let pets out whilst vocalizing. Dogs are extremely clever. They will associate this behavior with getting their own way. Remove all constricting articles such as collars or items when you leave your pup/dog in a crate.

Feed Meals in the Crate

Regular schedule should be maintained as you acclimate your pup by gradually lengthening their time alone in their crate. This slow pace is vital for their mental adjustment. When working towards achieving crate technique in stages, it will require that you feed puppies a meal inside the crate.

The crate method should never be used as an "out of sight, out of mind." Allow your pet to have plenty of breaks to extend their legs, bond, play, and enjoy family life. Once the eating session is over, place a chew toy along with the puppy inside the crate.

Throw the toy toward the far end of the crate. It could be a puzzle toy or a toy filled with some cheese spread. Puppies will work diligently for lengths of time to clean out all the goodies.

Leave the Door Open

If "time-out" is over, but your fur child is still playing with their toy, leave them inside and open the door but keep a close eye on them, so they don't explore elsewhere.

Crate your dog when you leave, you can leave pets for a total of one to two hours during the day, animals shouldn't spend any more time confined. Crate training is an optional method, and you can leave it out completely, but at times it's an extremely useful tool to have when you are needing it.

Dog crate training is also a crucial step toward having a well-mannered dog who uses the restroom outside and doesn't destroy things. Your dog will have a secure environment and its own personal space when kept in a crate.

Crate Your Dog at Night

Many dogs also need to learn how to unwind mentally instead of just passing out from exhaustion. You can teach your dog to unwind both inside and outside of a crate. The method still applies if you want to teach relaxation on a bed as opposed to a crate.

The same method can be used to teach your dog to relax in the car or any other setting where you want them to feel at ease and secure. The purpose of this training is to establish an association between your dog and calmness, relaxation, and security rather than simply teaching them to tolerate an enclosure.

Nip Crate Whining in the Bud

Puppies that are under six months old, shouldn't stay in a crate more than three to four hours. This will include toilet breaks. They are still learning how to control their bladders, so, keep time increments short when housetraining. Adult dogs who have been housebroken may be able to wait until they need to go potty, but they should never be contained for more than a few hours at a time.

Make the time in a crate enjoyable for your pet so that you have the best results. Your pet will develop a fear of containment and will refuse to enter a crate if you have misused its purpose. Make the transition to a new crate rewarding by doing so gradually.

Nothing is more upsetting than when a crate turns out to be a torture chamber and it was designed to be a happy retreat. The good news is that there are many things you can do to stop crate whining before it becomes a persistent issue.

Your dog should eventually 'cave' in and develop a love for its crate, given time and practice. But it's best to take it slow! Dogs are naturally den creatures, and they enjoy having a place to call home.

The best dog crates have dividers, so you can increase the size of the crate as your fur baby grows. This will avoid the need to buy a new crate as your dog ages. You will save money in the long run.

It will also give you the opportunity to design a space that feels both cozy and spacious at different stages of its development. Below are a few ideas you can incorporate to make a cage experience more tolerable.

Make Your Puppy Tired Before Crating

Playtime is one of the most effective tools to get your puppy to stop whining in their crate because a tired puppy tends to sleep in their cage. If you have placed your cage: in a busy location where all the action is, the next option would be to keep your puppy in the same room as you are when you sleep. You might consider buying two crates and keeping one near the end of your bed while you sleep.

Location Is Important

Not only will you hear when your pet needs to be let outside to use the restroom, but it will also make your pup feel less lonely and insecure. Create a space that is cozy for your puppy. This will encourage them to want to enter because it makes them feel warm and welcomed.

Purchase a Dog Bed That Is Comfy

Purchase a comfy dog bed and use a blanket and cushions to start with. Donut-style options are an excellent choice because they have higher sides than other designs, and this can help imitate the warmth of your dog's mother, which can be very comforting for a new pup.

Toys Are a Joy

After deciding on a bed, think about adding some toys that will help the puppy with its developing adult teeth. Plush toys are also a great addition because they are perfect for cuddling with.

Leash Training

Leash training can be challenging, but it's a skill you will need if you and your dog want to go on walks and adventures together. You should begin honing in on the skill as soon as you bring your new furry bundle home.

Introduce Puppy to Leash and Harness

Before trying to walk your dog, let them become accustomed to wearing a collar, leash, and harness. Let your pet walk the leash that is fastened to its collar all around the house.

While you play with your pup, give it a treat inside the house, and allow him to wear the items for brief intervals. The puppy should enjoy spending time with the collar and leash because it is associated with fun and food. You want them to feel at ease and not threatened by it.

Leash Training During Potty Time With the Treat Method

Leash training using an incentive method with the aid of treats. When you get close to your puppy, hold the leash in a loose loop position and give them a few treats in succession for standing or sitting beside you:

- As they catch up to you, give them another tasty treat to encourage them to follow you as you move forward.
- When you lead, keep rewarding your dog with treats at the same height as your knee or hip.
- Simply walk in the opposite direction, call your pet, and turn around if you see him running ahead of you. Reward him when he comes back to his spot.
- At this point, you can gradually expand the gap between treats.

By now, you should have reduced a large amount of treats and troubleshooting during walk time. Always have some treats on hand to reinforce good leash walking behavior.

Teach a Cue

Introduce a sound cue that signifies "food is coming" to your puppy. Some people enjoy clicking and treating, using the word 'yes,' and some enjoy clucking with their tongues. Regardless of the tool or cue, the process is the same: Make the noise while the puppy is on a leash and wearing a collar in a quiet, distraction-free area.

Give your puppy a treat as soon as he looks your way or turns to face you. After a few attempts, you will see that your puppy is approaching you for the treat as well as simply looking at you.

Practice Inside

Take your pup for a short stroll around the house or backyard to get them accustomed to the smells. They won't be as likely to wander off in a dozen different directions in search of intriguing new smells in this way.

Take Your Pup Outside

When you are finally prepared to put your puppy's skills to work in nature. The first step will present a set of new challenges because your puppy will hear sounds and smells and see fascinating sights. Keep the first walks brief and learn to practice patience.

If your puppy appears to be about to lunge toward something or become distracted while you're out for a walk. Make your cue sound and take a few steps back. Then give it a treat as a thank you, for following you.

Avoid "leveling up" too quickly, or moving from the backyard to a busy street during rush hour.

Before moving to a busy sidewalk, some dog owners find it helpful to use an 'intermediate' location, such as a courtyard or parking lot. Try to gradually increase the level of distraction by beginning your walk on a quiet street, early in the morning and work your way up to a busier location.

Praise Good Behavior

Give your dog lots of praise and give them treats occasionally when they 'heal' alongside you while on a loose leash. Never drag your dog behind you by pulling on the lead, you could potentially hurt your pet in this way.

Instead, concentrate on encouraging them to continue walking, while giving them a reward when they come to you. If they are especially persistent, you might need to step in and refocus their attention on walking rather than smelling the intriguing object that they are busy with.

Keep to the Boundaries

Your puppy will have the boundaries it needs, which will make both of you incredibly happy and content. Therefore, by not establishing boundaries, you prevent your pet honing its inherent dog skills.

Dogs are playful creatures who possess intelligent abilities that come from within and that can be developed upon. Emergency situations will benefit from these newly acquired skills.

Practice the 'Heel'

Practice the 'heel' command inside and outside your residence, and keep the puppy at your side. To teach heel, lower a treat to your dog's nose as you take a few steps forward. As they get accustomed to walking close to you, tag them with a word, and give them the treat as a reward. Reposition them next to you if they begin to pull or amble around.

Give Puppy Time to Do Its Business

If you train your puppy to potty on a leash, they should go naturally on walks. Let your pet relieve itself when you go out for walks. Make sure to take a pooper scooper and bags along so you can collect the mess and discard it later.

Walk in Different Environments

Your dog depends on you to walk them in exciting locations so they can experience the sights, sounds, and smells of the outside world. For this reason, it's a good idea to spread out where you take your dog as much as possible.

However, certain groups of dogs walk and socialize with each other on particular days in certain areas. If your pet has found a friend on a Monday and Friday for instance, walk them there on that route on those days.

Find a Pace

Puppies will walk at a certain pace and reach a limit, and, at times, you may need to pick them up and carry them. But with dogs, you can set a pace that you feel comfortable maintaining; for most dogs, this is between 15 and 19 minutes per mile. You ought to start to perspire lightly, and you should feel that you have had a brisk walk.

Remarkable Dogs Stories

The Story of Belle

Belle is a 17-pound beagle and she is more than just her owner's best friend; she's his lifesaver. Belle was living with her owner in Washington, D.C. at the time. One Monday, Belle made an award-receiving bite on her owner's cell phone to get it to call 911. This was after her owner had shown diabetic signs, which quickly progressed to a seizure and collapsing.

"There is no doubt in my mind that I'd be dead if I didn't have Belle," said Kevin Weaver, who is 34 years old. Kevin's blood sugar dropped drastically low, Belle noticed the signs and remembered her training on how to call for help. Her training included biting down on a number 9 on her owner's cell phone, which was coded to ring 911.

Animals like Belle have a good sense of smell and can identify changes in human blood sugar levels. Weaver's blood sugar is periodically measured by Bella when she licks his nose.

She will paw and whimper at him if something seems strange to her. Belle is the first canine to win the VITA Wireless Samaritan Award. This award is often given to a person who has used a cell phone to save a life, prevent crimes, or just to help with an emergency (Tarver, 2006).

Wrapping It Up

- Animals are natural den creatures, and a crate can also become their norm
- Create a command to enter a cage and encourage your pup to go in with treats
- Be patient as you gradually lengthen crate activity
- Never punish by using time in a crate.
- A puppy should spend more than 1 to 2 hours at a time in a crate
- Stay close to the crate when the crate door is open
- Take time to get the puppy used to a leash
- Practice inside the house first
- Make your outings exciting
- Walks will give you both an enjoyable work out

Your dog will develop positive interactions with certain situations that might otherwise have overwhelmed them. If you walk slowly and have fun, you will both enjoy yourselves. Whenever you train your puppy, remember that going slow and being patient are incredibly important.

Chapter 6:
Communication and Socialization

"Remember practice builds confidence. Practice with your pet, behaviors you want to see more of in different environments and with different reinforcements." (Unknown, 2020)

Understanding Your Puppy's Communication

Puppies have feelings that are comparable to ours, but they cannot express those feelings. Body language, behavior, or even physical well-being are outlets for expressing their emotions.

Believe it or not, particular behaviors that denote happiness, anxiousness, fear, confidence, and aggressiveness in puppies. Below are behavior signs to help you read these different behaviors:

When Your Puppy Is Happy

- When a puppy is joyful, their entire body will appear relaxed, and their tail will frequently wag! A dog that is wriggling and exposing its belly to you is probably (this can mean submission) very content and happy

- A soft, half-opened mouth
- Ears that are not drawn back or tense from alertness
- With a raised head, relaxed tail, and assured stance, the dog has a generally relaxed posture
- Making a "play bow," which involves lowering their chest and raising their rear as a request to play

By simply meeting a dog's basic physical, mental, and emotional needs it will keep them content. Make sure they eat well, get enough exercise, have enough mental stimulation, and receive a lot of affection and love.

When Your Puppy Is Anxious

Once a dog has anxiety and it's hard-wired in the brain, it's not easy to remove it. It's important to try and prevent rather than cure in this case. However, dogs have overcome anxiety with persistent work and help from their owner and professionals. In serious cases, dogs have needed medication to ease their nerves. Below are symptoms of anxious behavior:

- A puppy that has a stiff stance and wags its tail tautly may be alert or anxious
- Shivering
- Digging and getting out of the yard
- Running away or hiding in a corner of a house
- Taking apart furniture
- Eating stops
- If their owner is not home, the dog will bark or howl often

- Self-injury, such as excessive licking or chewing
- Pacing and panting (even in cool weather)
- Can't settling down
- Frequent urination

When Your Puppy Is Scared

Fear can be very debilitating to a pet in general, and this comes through its behavioral signs. Body language depicting fear might well be brought on by unsettling situations or people. It can extend to other animals that don't respect the puppy's space or it may just be a prolonged loud noise. Below are a few behavioral signs of fear:

- Dogs that avoid making eye contact with a scary person and turn their head away
- They yawn and cower and have rounded ears. The tail may have piloerection (hair standing on end) anywhere from their shoulder blades to the base of their tail
- A tense or hunched body that may also be shaking
- Whenever a dog's eye moves in the opposite direction of its head, and the whites are clearly visible, this is known as "whale eye"
- Lip licking
- Hiding or making an effort to get away
- Tail tucked in between the hind leg
- Nervous, frequent scratching

When Your Puppy Is Confident

Dogs and puppies will have a prideful walk when they are confident because they know they are a leader or the strongest sibling in a litter. They have nothing to prove to anyone as they know they don't have competition. They have no reason to be afraid of anyone.

They feel assured, and they can afford to be at ease with everyone. A confident dog often looks so relaxed that they seem docile, perhaps even uninterested. They can defend themselves effectively if necessary, but they only ever exert their dominance as a last resort.

Ironically, because they are calm and relaxed, you won't necessarily notice that your dog is confident. They are slow to react to even the most provocative triggers.

They show signs that they are happy and content because all the dogs around them know they are the boss. Like confident people, they become less reactive as their confidence grows.

When a Puppy Is Being Aggressive

Aggressiveness is often a byproduct of fear, an animal will show aggressive behavior to stop being attacked by a person or another dog. Much like, 'defense' is better than 'attack.' People have chemical imbalances in their make-up, and so do animals, and medication may rectify this imbalance.

There are a few exceptions to aggression, but it is mostly fueled by fear, and professionalism is advised. Below are a few behavioral signs of a dominant or aggressive dog:

- Staring, excessive low-range barking, snarling, growling, and snapping
- Standing tall, holding their ears up, and/or carrying the tail up high and moving stiffly from side to side. Be careful though, as aggressive, dominant dogs frequently don't show any warning before biting

Show That You Are in Charge During Communication

Even though dogs cannot speak, they can understand what you are saying. Behaviorist Dr. Stanley Coren claims that a canine is capable of learning approximately 165 words, and with intensive training, they can learn even more. Additionally, they are picking up on your tone of voice, to the words you are saying, and the body language you are portraying (Day, 2022).

In a recent experiment, scientists from the Universities of Lyon and St. Etienne discovered that puppies react favorably to higher-pitched recorded voices of a woman. Even adult dogs gravitated toward the recordings of high-pitched voices, but this didn't pique their interest for very long. This is because the person speaking wasn't physically present and interacting with the dogs (Day, 2022).

Humans are primates who touch, hug, like to make hand gestures, and speak in a loud, high-pitched voice when they are upset or excited. All of these situations are perplexing and can mean danger, particularly to puppies.

Use a Calm Voice

Use a sweet, higher-pitched calm voice and clipped sentences. Routine is ideal for puppies to convey the meaning of words by using the same cue word so that the action will merge with the word.

Avoid Yelling and Looming

When you are upset with the behavior of your dog, yelling the word 'no,' won't result in a positive change in their behavior.

The pet can clearly see that you are upset, and they may show signs of anxiety, but they often don't understand why you are upset. All they hear is anger and rage, and they will often flee from the situation.

So, don't yell but say in a stern voice 'no,' and point to the action that you are not happy with. Now, show them what should have happened or clean up the unrolled toilet roll that is all over the place.

Humans are taller than puppies, and it is normal to stoop down to talk to our pets. To a dog, however, 'looming' over the top means 'I'm the boss, I'm in control,' which can make them apprehensive. Puppies who already respect you as the pack leader may find that upsetting or even frightening. They may demonstrate threat behavior by making appeasement gestures like submissive wetting.

Use Hand Signals or Body Gestures

Since they use body language to interact with other dogs in packs and in social settings, dogs are experts at interpreting and observing body language.

When teaching puppies to sit, the open-hand signal is effective. Every time you say 'sit,' just open your hand, and your dog will learn that the action itself serves as a command. In time, all you will need to do to get your dog to sit is to open your hand.

Show Your Puppy How to Behave

By teaching your dog to sit before jumping on house guests or other visitors and keeping your dog on a leash, is a successful start to your training. Requesting that the visitors arrive calmly and gradually, you can set the puppy up for success. Give your fur child a treat for good behavior, and only permit visitors to pet your fur bundle when it's calm and when all four paws are on the ground.

Speak Less

Let the treats speak for themselves! Your dog will become more perplexed the more you converse with them or use different words. The simplest verbal cue to use when teaching your dog commands is to say it just once, followed only if necessary.

Avoid the urge to rephrase or repeat the verbal cue continually. Your dog won't understand any better if you say 'Come' instead of 'Get over here, little fellow' or 'Come on over.'

Most talking is done between humans, so you should be aware that your dog will tune out the majority of what you say. Those vocalizations used by humans have nothing to do with how dogs communicate and are probably ignored.

Increase Expectations

Increase the length of your training sessions or the time your dog spends practicing a skill if you notice that they are starting to get the hang of it.

For instance, when you teach your pup to 'stay,' releasing your pup from this position, within a half-second or one treat. Then work gradually for half a second, and after that, reward them with two treats. Eventually, when they show signs of understanding, decrease the frequency of treats. This will determine if your dog has perfected the skill without the need for rewards.

Use the Leash

One of the most effective means of communication between dogs and people may be the leash. Dogs are experts at interpreting our emotions, and the leash acts as a bridge between our bodies and theirs.

You will probably tighten up on your leash if you are anxious or under stress, by shortening the distance between your hand and the dog. The leash will probably be held loosely if you are feeling carefree. If you have time for a leisurely walk, your pace will be slow; if you are in a hurry, you might tug on the leash more frequently when your dog stops to sniff around.

When you approach a noisy construction site or a group of barking dogs behind a fence, assurance and reassurance are shown in your body language. The leash handling they experience will make them less fearful.

Don't Use Pain to Teach

The leash has effective power in itself without the aid of tools like choke, prong, or shock collars. Equipment that hurts is more likely to muddle your pets' understanding. Tools that inflict pain might communicate that it's the innocent dog that is passing who is inflicting the pain rather than the items listed.

For instance, a prong collar pushes hard metal dowels into my dog's neck when the pet pulls on the leash. The discomfort of metal tightening over their trachea will be felt if I have a dog that gets excited when they see other dogs, and I decide to pull slightly on its leash. This will now cause a socialization problem on top of the pain they have I have dealt to the poor animal.

The pet has no idea that the owner they trust is the one pulling on the leash and making them uncomfortable; all they know is that there's another dog nearby, and that hurts. The best way to use a leash is as a safety measure rather than as a training tool.

If you are calm and confident and convey your message to your dog through your voice and body language rather than an intimidating collar, they will understand what you are trying to say to them and they will learn.

Creating a Bond With Your Puppy

Getting a new puppy entails assuming new responsibilities and starting fresh relationships. Forming a bond with a pet can be a lot of fun, but it also requires a lot of effort. Making this effort can help you and your dog have a less stressful transition into pet ownership as well as prevent future headaches.

Establish Communication

As often as possible, consider combining a verbal cue with a body signal cue to improve communication with your dog. Interact with your puppy and strengthen your relationship.

Give Puppy Boundaries

Having clearly established boundaries and being consistent with your puppy promotes a stronger connection between the two of you. As their leader and someone they continue to look to for guidance, this is important.

Create a Daily Schedule

Have your schedule established and in place. The main components of planning your puppy's daily schedule are meals, playtime, potty breaks, and nap times. For your puppy to really get the hang of being a member of the family, try to stick as closely as you can to your regular schedule.

Make It a Game

Your puppy can learn to listen through initiated play. Additionally, it's enjoyable to connect with them by feeling their energy on the other end of the tug toy.

Another fantastic and constructive game to play fetch. Each of these activities helps a puppy learn that you are reliable or trustworthy while also stimulating their brains with fun.

Exercise Your Puppy

Although there are many advantages to exercise, it should all be done in moderation! Puppies can be very energetic, but too much exercise can harm their forming joints and increase their stamina. Consult your puppy's veterinarian when you go for puppy vaccines on how to start the puppy's daily activities to determine what safe pursuits your puppy can partake in.

Build Trust Through Cuddling and Handling

This entails getting your puppy accustomed to having their belly, ears, paws, legs, mouth, nose, tail, and behind touched.

If your puppy or dog is unaccustomed to being handled. Give your dog some of their food in one hand while starting to touch these areas with the other hand in a slow and gentle mannerism.

The ideal time to do this is when they are tired, keep rewarding them when they allow you to touch them. Light grooming procedures like brushing their fur or cleaning their eyes will work well too.

Be Patient

Each dog has a unique personality, and some dogs are slower to warm up to new people and environments than others. Dogs go through an adjustment period when put in a new situation, just like we do. Before we get into some of the fun ways to bond with your new puppy, I want to highlight how crucial it is to have patience.

Be Consistent

Punishing your dog for a behavior that you find objectionable but your husband support is unfair to your pet. Making sure that everyone in the family agrees on what behaviors are acceptable will help you avoid frustration. Positive reinforcement helps you to raise a balanced and happy pet.

Relax Together

Spend time with your puppy and watch a movie together or sit outside in the garden together in the cool sun or shade. Have a nap together on the carpet, but be warned, little ones can escape quietly.

Practice Hand-Feeding

Simply put, hand-feeding your dog means giving him food out of your hand. It's especially helpful for timid or fearful dogs. It's a good way to begin strengthening your bond with your dog and an exercise that will help you both to become more trusting of one another.

Work on Simple Tricks

Puppy training is a great way to develop a bond with your new dog because puppies aren't too young to learn some simple tricks. Just remember that they have a short attention span and to keep your training sessions brief. It's a good idea to start laying down the groundwork for a dependable recall because you will also want to teach your pup to respond well to cues when called.

Socialize Your Puppy With Other Humans and Dogs

As each new interaction offers positive reinforcement and experiences when you are socializing your pups, their confidence will undoubtedly increase. A puppy's first three months of life must include a period of socialization.

Introduce Your Puppy to a Wide Range of People

To help your dog become accustomed to the idea of people, expose them to a variety of different types of people, including men, women, and children. It's important to diversify your dog's social life and schedule meet-and-greets because if they only spend time with one person, they might become suspicious of anyone who isn't that person.

If your dog appears fearful, remain composed and assured. Avoid pushing or jerking on a leash, making a big deal out of skittish or timid behavior. People should only pet your fur baby if their hands are visible to the puppy, such as on the chest or chin of your dog. Treats can help your dog form positive associations with different people and situations.

Carry a Lot of Treats

You will know your dog's preferences best when deciding on a treat. Tasty, high-value treats will last longer. Dogs frequently enjoy string cheese, cooked chicken bits, and tiny pieces of hard-boiled eggs. Always remember to alter your dog's meal time calorie intake to make up for the extra calories at snack time.

Make sure that interactions you meet along the way last long enough to get to know other animals and people but not so long that they exhaust your fur baby. Even though it might sound adorable to introduce a three-pound chihuahua to a great dane, always proceed with caution.

Before arranging a meet and sniff, always make sure the other party is cordial. I have heard that some pet owners carry pieces of hotdog around with them to get rid of the approach of an aggressive dog.

Family Involvement

The whole family should become involved in raising your fur baby. Make it a fun activity for the kids by asking them to create a list of all the new things the puppy saw or heard while with them that day, such as someone in a baseball cap or a police siren.

Take it slow and avoid taking on too much at once. For instance, start with a few family members and gradually introduce one stranger, then two, and so on until your puppy is comfortable being handled by multiple strangers. Starting this process off by bringing your puppy to a loud party or a crowded public area can be stressful and result in a future fear of crowds and strangers.

How to Stop a Puppy From Biting

You must identify any early indications of aggression or annoyance towards situations as some of the best-behaved canines occasionally bite people. Any dog can act aggressively if they are fearful of something. It's important to act quickly and find help in getting to the root of the problem.

While a muzzle shouldn't be used in place of training, it will stop your dog from biting in a fearful situation or from eating inappropriate items while out on a walk. If you are worried about your dog in public, always keep them on a lead and consider muzzling, until you sort the problem out.

Training School

Your puppy can enroll in puppy classes once its vaccinations have begun. The most significant benefit of these classes is that they introduce your puppy to other dogs and people, which goes beyond just helping them start to understand simple commands.

The meetings will be mediated by knowledgeable trainers to ensure the safety and happiness of both people and dogs throughout. Local AKC training clubs and dog training facilities may offer puppy classes in your area.

Dog school is another option and this is offered by Dogs Trust, and this is an enjoyable training program that is rewarding to both dog owner and pet. These classes assist owners in interpreting their dog's behavior and in teaching them coping mechanisms. This will help them adjust to life at home and deal with everyday situations.

A better bond can be established, and fewer behavioral problems will result from helping people notice some of the more subtle ways dogs communicate with us.

Biting and Rough Play

Biting and rough play are typical behaviors that puppies display, so punishment won't work. It is important to inform owners that puppies must learn to control their biting, a process that starts with their younger siblings.

Once the puppies are at their owner's house, this same reinforcement should continue.

Rough play, biting, mouthing, and chewing on inappropriate objects are all unacceptable behaviors when used on people. Puppy inhibition is the process by which it learns to control the force of its actions. Puppies learn through play and by biting and being bitten, and through time spent with their siblings; this teaches them to be aware of when they bite too hard.

Puppies begin to understand that when the hard bit is given back, it hurts. They quickly pick up on the ability to pause, modify the force of their bite, and soften the impact of their bite so that play can resume. It cannot be overstated enough, that to redirect your dog's attention, buy suitable chew toys or even make your own toys so that your dog will be focused on them instead of you.

Now is the time to act responsibly and set up procedures to protect your puppy and yourself because we know that puppies will develop into adult dogs, and behavioral issues may arise.

Remarkable Dogs Stories

A Story About Dexter

An Alsatian and military working canine named Dexter has saved over a thousand lives during his tours on duty, going to Iraq, Afghanistan, and other places. In one particular heroic case, Dexter was patrolling the streets of Baghdad when he discovered explosives in a garbage truck that was going to blow up at an American mess hall; he saved hundreds of soldiers' lives that day.

At the age of 10, Dexter nearly missed out on his retirement. Due to acquiring a hip injury and the fact that most military and police dogs are too aggressive to be adopted. His Navy handler Kathleen Ellison begged congressmen to save this heroic dog's life.

Ellison managed to reach out to Debbie Kandoll, the owner of Military Working Dog Adoptions, who introduced her to Danny Scheurer, a co-founder of Save-A-Vet and an Iraq War veteran.

Post commander Jerry Kandziorski stated that he believed that Dexter should be admitted without question. "We feel he is a military veteran. He deserves some recognition of his own," Kandziorski explained. "He spent six years in Iraq, and he deserves this."

Dexter arrived in Spring Grove, for a public ceremony at Fox Lake American Legion Post 703, where he was welcomed and praised. Dexter was also given a place to live out the remainder of his golden years in luxury with harmony and love. As a veteran of the American Legion (Bartosik, 2008).

Wrapping it Up

- It is vital to understand your dog/puppy and recognize behavioral signs
- Use a calm, high sweet voice and don't yell at them
- Use cue words and hand signals as well as body gestures
- Speak less and treat more
- Owner tend to exhibit fear and anxiety when they walk with their dog a leash
- Increase expectations slowly
- It's vital to create a bond with your pet
- Lay down boundaries and keep to a daily schedule
- Build trust through games and being patient
- Be relaxed but consistent
- Encourage positive behavior
- Socialize our pet from an early age
- Stock up on treats
- Act quick when witnessing warning signs in your pet

By socializing your puppy, you enable them to become open to a whole new, and exciting world.

Chapter 7:
Puppy Training 101

"Always give your dog the benefit of the doubt." (Deeley, 2020)

No matter how adorable our furry children are, they are still not going to be perfect at everything. They may be in the trash, they could pull off tablecloths, or eat a leg off the coffee table, and they might even destroy your brand-new, pricey, and comfortable slippers. I'm sorry to break it to you, but puppies don't have any common sense, and they have no idea what they did was wrong.

The most essential thing is to first acknowledge your mistakes in your puppy's training and rectify those errors as fast as you can. Continue to work toward your ultimate goal of owning the brainiest puppy/dog in town. At the very least, you can have a reasonably well-trained dog that knows how to use the bathroom and displays positive behavior when it's necessary.

Mistakes People Make

Puppy training is far more successful if you take away anything that your puppy shouldn't have and give them what they can have. Puppies are highly motivated when you use a reward and this will give them an incentive to remember what they have learned.

You should do everything in your power to help your puppy succeed when it goes through its learning phase. This is when they learn what they can and cannot chew and will last for at least the first year of its life.

Never Leave Your Pet in a Vehicle

Never leave your pets in a vehicle and think that a window left ajar will make a difference. According to a study published in the journal Pediatrics, the temperature inside your car rises quickly to over 115 degrees on a mild day of about 70 degrees Fahrenheit; the majority of these heat changes occur within 30 minutes.

Additionally, even when their body temperature is just 103 degrees, dogs can develop heat exhaustion and die. So, don't leave your pets in a vehicle, even if it's only for a moment (Marie, 2019).

Never Let Your Puppy Lead You

You can establish yourself as the pack leader by walking in front of your dog. On the other hand, your dog is the pack leader if he dominates you while out for a walk. Pets will stop respecting you and believe that they are in control if you allow it.

You ought to be the first person in and the first person out of the room. During the walk, your dog should be by your side at 'heel' or towards the rear.

People Don't Neuter and Spay Their Animals

Female dogs who are spayed are less likely to develop breast cancer and have no chance of developing uterine or ovarian cancer. The prevalence of prostate cancer is also decreased by neutering male dogs. Neutered animals are less likely to wander, engage in conflict, and produce unwanted litters.

Dogs don't like a Pat on the Head, Hugs, or Kisses

Although some people disagree, most experts concur with Coren's analyst analysis. This analysis states that dogs: do not enjoy being hugged as the action immobilizes them, resulting in high levels of anxiety and stress, which might, in extreme cases, result in aggression or biting, or just a nervous disposition.

Kissing is seen and understood as licking and a dog starts to categorize you as one of the pack, rather than their owner. Patting can be recognized as a threat and can create an aggressive dog.

Sarah Bartlett, a qualified international dog training instructor, told The Mirror that it was wrong to approach a dog and lean in and pat or stoke them on the head. So, show your kids other ways to love their puppies and avoid any problems later.

Consoling Your Puppy

It may come as a shock to you to learn this, and I know you will find it difficult to resist, but comforting your puppy after a tense situation is strictly forbidden. Showering them with affection and love: after they run and hide underneath the bed, whine, or display fear is simply not something that should be done, whether it's a loud noise, a new person, or a new situation.

Your precious pet will become confused and begin to mistake acting scared for receiving attention, which is something you definitely don't want. If this behavior persists, your dog is more likely to develop a perpetually anxious attitude, and it might turn into an aggressive adult. We want our fur children to become as well-rounded and, hopefully, fearless and content as they can be.

Scolding Well After the Mess Occurred

You discover a mess in the hallway, and you make up your mind on how it got there. You scold your puppy for making the mess as it approaches you with her tail wagging. Why is this image flawed?

Many dogs (especially puppies) don't understand why they are being punished or shouted at for something that happened an hour ago. Puppies have a poor sense of time, and all you accomplish in the mind of a pet is the impression that you are irate whenever waste is present.

Puppies will become secretive about eliminating as a result, which will disrupt their housetraining. Say nothing to your dog; an accident that is discovered after the fact is an accident that is too late to be discovered. Instead, until they are reliable, reduce their independence, use the crate, and clean up the mess thoroughly.

Key In Solving Problems and Daily Training Tips

Recall

Dog recall works when the idea of going back to the owner is more alluring than a potential distraction. This training will have to override your pet's innate desire to chase anything it sees. To achieve this you will need to combine the use of incentives and constructive criticism.

Establishing and maintaining a reliable recall is essential, as without mastering this training, your puppy cannot spend time off its leash, which could be harmful. They might socialize with other dogs during this time, or you might have to call them away from potential or unexpected danger.

Come

The word 'come' is another crucial command for your pet to learn. If you slip up and let go of the leash or forget to latch the front door, this command will be handy. Simply use this command as a teaching aid to help keep your pet in line.

You want to encourage your fur member to come back, so keep your voice upbeat and refrain from sounding frustrated. Never make coming back to you feel like such a punishment; your puppy should never experience stress or anxiety!

This should be a fun and stimulating experience. When your pup loses focus during training, stop immediately and try again later. Below are a few steps to follow:

- Pick a place that is peaceful and uncluttered, and free of any distractions.
- Put your puppy on a short leash and call the puppy's name. If your dog stares or looks at you when you call their name, that is a clear indication that they are responding well. Don't forget to show them some love or affection when they do something correctly.
- Keep in mind that puppies have a limited attention span; therefore, keep your sessions brief and end them when your puppy is still eager to learn more rather than when it's mentally worn out.
- When wanting your puppy to 'come,' back up a few steps as he approaches you while still wearing the leash and collar, and praise them

when they approach you. Continue practicing until your puppy comes to you and walks a short distance with you in response to the cue noise.

- As soon as your pup approaches you, reward it and this is cause for a celebration. You could use a whistle, clicker, or any other sound that your pet will associate with the command 'come,' and always reward them for their obedience. Maintain the training for at least six to eight weeks, repeat this exercise every time you go for a walk, and gradually lengthen the lead until it reaches the recommended 30 feet.

- Take your puppy further away to more of an open area, such as a park. The true test to see if they have mastered the skill is when they return to you.

- You could continue to further advance their recall skills to the point where they will come back to you regardless of the distance.

No or Leave It!

You might not want your dog to consume anything that would be harmful to their digestive system. This is why using the commands 'no' or "leave it" is beneficial. Below are a few steps you can follow:

- Hold treats in both hands. Move the first treat or hand slowly toward your dog's face to get them to lick or sniff it before giving the command to "leave it" or 'no.'

- Whenever your dog tries to take the first treat out of your hand, resist the urge to give it to them. Once your dog no longer shows any interest in the first treat, give the second treat from the opposite hand. When they demonstrated the desired behavior by taking the option. Make sure your dog practices the exercise until he or she is proficient at it.

Sit

The 'sit' command is one of the easiest dog commands to teach, so it's a good place to start. A dog that has mastered the command 'sit' will calm down and become much easier to handle than one who has not.

Additionally, 'sit' prepares your dog for even more challenging commands like 'stay' and 'come.' How to teach your dog to 'sit' is as follows:

- Keep a treat near your dog's nose at all times. When you raise your hand, let the animal's bottom drop down so that its eyes follow the treat as its head moves backward.
- When your pet is sitting, command 'Sit,' provide the treat, and lavish your pet with love to express your gratitude.

Stay

Stay is similar to the 'sit' command, the 'stay' command will assist you in keeping your dog under control and secure in specific circumstances. This command can be useful in a variety of circumstances, such as avoiding a vehicle that is approaching your property or preventing overcrowding among your guests.

Make sure your puppy is familiar with the 'sit' command before attempting to teach them the 'stay' command. Therefore, practice the 'sit' command for a while before switching to 'stay.' Below are a few steps you can follow:

- Start by telling your dog to 'sit' and then tell them to 'stay' and then turn your palm over to face your animal. If your pet stays still while you take a few steps back and move slowly, praise and reward them.
- Before giving the treat, gradually extend the distance. Give your dog treats each time it stays, even if it only stays for a short while.

You can use this as a self-control exercise. A lot of the time, especially with puppies and high-energy dog breeds, it takes some time to master. In addition, the majority of dogs prefer to 'walk' rather than the command 'stay.'

Drop It

Teaching the command drop can be a little challenging, but with a bit of effort on your part, you will master the skill. Below are a few steps to follow:

- When your dog opens their mouth and shows a willingness to grab or catch the object, give the command "take it" to initiate the action.
- After giving them some time to play with the object, gradually introduce a second object that is exactly like the first one. Once your dog moves forward and grabs the second object, it gives the impression that it has equal value for both.
- Now is the moment to give the command "drop it" after your dog has dropped the first object.
- When your dog catches or grabs the second object, say the command "take it." Reward your dog for good behavior and repeat the exercise until it becomes second nature.

Corrective Anxiety Training

If you have a pet that becomes anxious if left alone, you need to start teaching your fur baby that it has nothing to fear. Start by following this method I have set out for you and work from there.

- Go to the door after putting your shoes on. Try to ignore your dog's panicking, so they become accustomed to this action. Do this at least three times each day.
- When you return home, hold off on greeting your dog at the door right away. By doing this, you will be telling your puppy that coming home is something that will be happening regularly.

- Not something to be happy about even though you know in your heart it is!

When you get home, tell your dog to go to bed. After they comply with your instructions and quiet down, extend a calm welcome and allow them to sense your affection. Dogs that overreact when visitors arrive or leave the house frequently pick up this behavior from family members who put on elaborate emotional displays whenever they come or go.

The dog eventually becomes vocal and agitated whenever the door is opened. Instead, whenever you have to leave your puppy, just do it quietly. The same is true when you arrive; remain silent for a moment, until the puppy settles down a little. Next, greet her, draw her attention with a treat, and give her praise.

Corrective Food Aggression Training

A training program can be used to train against food aggression in puppies or dogs. Here we will be using multiple counter-conditioning techniques to focus on desensitization. This will help your pet to become more comfortable eating near people or other animals.

- When your fur baby is eating, you must become available. During this phase, your puppy will get used to your appearance while they are occupied with treats or meals. Dogs, like any other pet, can be territorial, and this can be directed toward their food. Animals that are aggressive toward their food become overly protective of it. This is a problem for several reasons, including the possibility of bites from people living with the dog and your pet acting clingy in other situations.

- Expand on the first action by attempting to place a tasty treat inside your puppy's bowl and quickly retreat to your starting location or distance. Don't give up; the value of consistency cannot be overstated.

- Decide to move one step forward every day until you are now standing two steps away from the dog's dish. Make sure that you do this within 10 feedings.

- Stand next to your dog while they eat from their bowl and give them a special treat. Talk to them in a conversational manner and ask questions like, "What's that in your dish?" or "How's it tasting?" Start to move away from your dog once you have given them the treat. The process should be repeated every few seconds.

- Approach your dog and talk to it in a conversational manner, just as you did in the previous step. Holding out your hand with a treat toward your dog, stand next to their bowl. Encourage your dog to eat the treat out of your hand rather than placing it in their bowl.

- Turn around as soon as they take the treat to help them understand that you are not interested in their food. Each day, try to stoop down even closer until your hand is directly next to their bowl so that your pet can take the treat.

- Talk to them in a low, friendly voice as you give your pet the treat. Do not take food from their bowl. Only touch it with your other hand. This will make it easier for your dog to get used to your presence at mealtimes. If your pet continues to be calm while eating for a period of ten consecutive meals, move on to the next phase of training.

- Since you will be lifting their bowl off the ground to give your pet a treat, this stage is essential for developing trust. Speak calmly to your pet when you pick up their bowl.
- Place the bowl back on the ground after adding the treat and lifting it 6 to 12 inches. Try every day to raise the bowl a little higher until you can set it down on a table to prepare the treat. Repeat this procedure until you can move a short distance away and take their bowl with you. Walk back and put your dog's bowl back where you found it.

Your pet will gain knowledge and trust and feel confident in obeying you as a result, and the trust will grow. When your dog is hungry, all it may want is to feel at ease and not be threatened by losing its meal. A regular feeding schedule might have been all this dog ever needed in the first place. If your efforts fail, however, you should consult your veterinarian or a nearby trainer.

Remarkable Dogs Stories

A Story About Todd a Golden Retriever

Todd, a golden retriever, earned the title of hero because he risked his life to defend his owner. On Friday, June 29, Todd jumped in front of Paula Godwin's leg as they were walking down a hill in Anthem, Arizona, protecting her from a rattlesnake bite.

Godwin said, "As we were walking down the hill I literally stepped on a rattlesnake. But my hero puppy Todd saved me. He bolted to my leg," she told the BBC. "That's when he was bitten by the snake. Todd was yelping right away. Crying, I picked him up, ran down the hill with my other dog Copper, and we got him to the hospital within 10 minutes of being bitten."

"He got the anti-venom quickly and was in the hospital for about 12 hours. He surely saved me from being bitten. He's my hero." Todd never considered the consequences, and it didn't matter how injured Todd would be as long as he was able to save his beloved Godwin from the snake (Mearns, 2018).

Wrapping It Up

- We should realize that puppies don't know right from wrong and that it is our job to teach them
- Safety comes first. Never leave your pet in a vehicle
- Be aware of your animal's behavior, and you must lead your dog when walking

- Dogs don't like to be hugged, kissed, or patterned
- Never scold your puppy once the potty is done
- Don't console your puppy after they have hidden under a chair
- Start training animal immediately and keep an upbeat attitude

Wherever we go, we always want to have a good relationship with our canine companions. Teaching your puppy these basic commands to address any behavioral problems will ensure a healthy and happy companionship. Be consistent and patient, and your puppy will learn it all.

Conclusion

I'm quite confident that everything will go well for you and your four-legged member. I do not doubt that if you make the right decision on a puppy or dog and follow my recommendations, you will have a loving, well-balanced companion in your life.

There are many reasons to love dogs, besides their boisterousness and curious attitude, their friendship and unconditional love are far the most precious. Dogs are so vital in our lives, whether they are just waiting at the door when you get home or when you are giggling happily after an entertaining game or walking with them. You can trust that your devoted companion will always be there to lift your spirits when things are at their worst.

The majority of pet owners are not aware of the instant advantages received when having a furry child in their lives. Many don't realize the greater health benefits that pet owners acquire. These advantages that come through cuddling up to a furry bundle carry physical and emotional wellbeing.

Recent scientific research on the advantages of human-animal bonding has been conducted. Animals have developed a keen sensitivity to human behavior, emotions, and traits. Dogs, for instance, are excellent at reading nonverbal cues like our tone of voice and body language (Ross et al., 2014).

One of the reasons animals, especially dogs, have such therapeutic impacts on people is that they gratify a basic human desire for touch. In fact, many prisoners have felt the affections and are feeling compassion for one another for the first time.

When you reach out to touch an animal your feelings of worry or upset, will quickly be replaced by serenity or peace. Most canines serve as a good influence on healthy exercise, pet companionship can also relieve loneliness. Dogs definitely lift your spirits and lessen despair as we go through the trials of life with them (Walsh, 2009).

There is still a lot to owning a pet, as you can see when reading my book. It starts with selecting a professional breeder or finding the right match. Breeders set the tone by modeling certain behaviors in your puppy as they grow up.

Check all the breeders out carefully and ask people who have owned a particular breed that you are leaning towards. Go to the breeder's house and ask about their habits, and watch how they behave.

The dog breeder should give the puppies a lot of attention even when you visit them. The more positive the interactions it has, the more positive its personality will develop into. This will determine how it will respond to its new surroundings once it's a fully grown dog.

Some rescues might need a bit more time and effort to adjust, but, most of the time, they are so appreciative of your attention and love, and this, in itself, will become rewarding. It's also important for your puppy to maintain a healthy weight for the rest of its life.

While overweight puppies are more likely to grow up to be overweight adult dog; underweight puppies may not develop properly. Diabetes, heart disease, high blood pressure, arthritis, and heat exhaustion are just a few of the illnesses that can result from weight issues.

At each appointment, your veterinarian should assess your puppy's body condition score to make sure you are following the correct nutrition plan for your type of dog. Trial and error may be involved in training a pet, but with the resources that I have set out for you, you can be sure it's tried and tested, and the outcome will be well worth your while.

Accidents are inevitable, but you can share a tidy home with your puppy if you are consistent, patient, and provide lots of positive reinforcement. It all comes down to giving your dog the appropriate training and mix of toys to keep it amused and stimulate its mind, to ward against boredom.

Crate-trained dogs will not only significantly speed up potty training and prevent separation anxiety, but it may also make going to the groomer and the vet less traumatic by providing your pet with a secure, comfortable place to feel at home in.

Gently exposing puppies to a variety of situations will enable their success and determine their temperament over the long term. In addition to helping your dog become a well-adjusted canine citizen, exposing your pet to new people, places, dogs, animals, and experiences will help avoid any future exaggerated reactions from occuring. Therefore, through appropriate socialization and situation, anxiety can be prevented.

The ultimate goal of dog walking is to have your dog stay close to you, voluntarily rather than out of need. In order to make your dog happy, you must attend to their mental and physical requirements and comprehend what those needs are in the context of your dog's life.

For instance, don't allow your pet in situations that will create it to fail, and ensure their food is balanced, healthful, and appropriate for their stage of life and the needs they require. Groom and medicate your animal when needed, and allow for the comforts that will make them happy.

Give your fur child enough brain activity through exercise, games, such as chew toys, food puzzles, and training. Give them the right amount of physical activity for their age and stage of life. They should also be lavished with love and attention.

If you have ever had a puppy in your life, you have likely committed one or more classic errors when training, and that's completely acceptable! But now that you know exactly what to avoid, you can start teaching your dog some useful skills so that can prevent those plush slippers from being mauled by your puppy.

Happy exercise is crucial, but it's just as important to pay attention to your dog's emotional signs, observe adjustments in body language or behavior could point to emotional stress, discomfort from their surroundings, or even illness. However, it's also crucial to account for changes in their mood.

Aggression toward people or dogs is often the result of a lack of training and socialization, but it can also stem from past abuse. It is vital that you are recognized as a pack leader and that is simply to lead your dog and make them realize that your 'No' means 'No.'

The biggest problems are that a lot of individuals don't know how to lead their dogs or have no idea of what needs a dog requires. Instead, they give your dog human emotions and human food. Every dog is unique, and they all have their own histories and personalities. It may take your dog several weeks or even months to settle in and develop a bond with you, and that should be o.k.

Your new puppy will begin to feel at home in its new surroundings if you give it some time, consistency, a regular schedule, and its own place. Did you know that when children are young, caring for and being kind to animals can help them grow up to be more secure and sympathetic?

So, there are a lot of benefits to owning a dog, and all your dog needs are patience and optimism when tackling its training and requirements, and your new dog will quickly become your best bud and a member of your family.

References

ABC Net Staff. (2019, April 8). Should you cuddle a crying dog? Signs your pet is anxious and how to treat it. *ABC Net.* https://www.abc.net.au/everyday/signs-your-dog-is-anxious-and-how-to-treat-it/10952390

AKC Staff. (2021, August 20). Fruits & vegetables dogs can and can't eat. *American Kennel Club.* https://www.akc.org/expert-advice/nutrition/fruits-vegetables-dogs-can-and-cant-eat/

All Things Pups Staff. (2016, June 6). How to respond to your pup's accident. *All Things Pups®.* https://allthingspups.com/respondtopupsaccident/

Amanda. (2015, August 14). 10 most common choking hazards for dogs. *One Love Animal Rescue.* https://oneloveanimalrescue.com/10-most-common-choking-hazards-for-dogs/

Andes, A. (2017, November 2). How to safely socialize your new puppy with other dogs. *Peach on a Leash.* https://peachonaleash.com/how-to-safely-socialize-your-new-puppy-with-other-dogs/

ASPCA. (2021). Pet statistics. *ASPCA.* https://www.aspca.org/helping-people-pets/shelter-intake-and-surrender/pet-statistics

ASPCA Staff. (2015). Poisonous plants. *ASPCA.* https://www.aspca.org/pet-care/animal-poison-control/toxic-and-non-toxic-plants

AZ Animals Staff. (2022, May 26). The best puppy bowls. *AZ Animals.* https://a-z-animals.com/reviews/the-best-puppy-bowls/

Balabanov, I. (2022). Https://twitter.com/dogtrainersocal/status/1499200406034993153. Twitter. https://twitter.com/DogTrainerSoCal/status/1499200406034993153

Bartosik, M. (2008, December 19). Dexter the dog comes home a war hero. *NBC Chicago.* https://www.nbcchicago.com/local/an-iraq-war-hero-like-none-other/1850504/

Bender, A. (2021, April 3). How to tell if a dog is afraid. *The Spruce Pets.* https://www.thesprucepets.com/symptoms-of-fear-in-dogs-1117890

Beynen, A. (2017, January). Brain food for puppies. *ResearchGate.* https://www.researchgate.net/publication/312017422_Brain_food_for_puppies

Bond Vet Staff. (2019, May 23). Pee pads for puppies: The pros and cons. *Bond Vet.* https://bondvet.com/b/puppy-pee-pads

Bored Panda Staff. (2022, July 4). This blind dog has his own seeing-eye guide and they're looking for a home. *Bored Panda.* https://www.boredpanda.com/blind-dog-guide-best-friends-abandoned-rescued-stray-aid-shelter-glenn-buzz/?utm_source=google&utm_medium=organic&utm_campaign=organic

Caldwell, A. (2017, September 15). How to prevent your dog from getting worms. *Wag Walking.* https://wagwalking.com/wellness/how-to-prevent-your-dog-from-getting-worms

Cappiello, E. (2020, April 23). This is how much time you should spend with your dog, according to experts. *POPSUGAR Pets.* https://www.popsugar.com/pets/how-much-time-should-i-spend-with-my-dog-47351933

Cesar's Way Staff. (2019, September 19). The right shampoo for your dog. *Cesar's Way.* https://www.cesarsway.com/the-right-shampoo-for-your-dog/#:~:text=If%20you%27ve%20got%20a

Day, J. (2022, February 14). 7 tips for better communication with your canine. *Akcpet Insurance.* https://www.akcpetinsurance.com/blog/7-tips-for-better-communication-with-your-canine

Debbie. (2021, November 23). How to potty train a puppy in an apartment. *Puppy in Training.* https://puppyintraining.com/how-to-potty-train-a-puppy-in-an-apartment/

Deeley, M. (2020a, September 28). Always give your dog the benefit of the doubt. *Hepper*. https://www.hepper.com/dog-training-quotes/

Deeley, M. (2020b, September 28). When it comes to training a dog, 5 minutes a day monday through friday is better than 30 minutes on saturday. *Hepper*. https://www.hepper.com/dog-training-quotes/

Dobman, D. N. (2021, September 15). Puppy potty training schedule for the first-time dog parent. *Pet Place*. https://www.petplace.com/article/dogs/pet-care/house-training-schedules-for-puppies/

Dodman, D. N. (2015, August 25). Cleaning supplies you need when you have a puppy. *Petplace*. https://www.petplace.com/article/dogs/pet-care/cleaning-supplies-you-need-when-you-have-a-puppy/

Dog Tails Staff. (2014, August 18). The do's and don'ts of potty training your puppy. *Dog Tails*. https://dogtails.dogwatch.com/2014/08/18/the-dos-and-donts-of-potty-training-your-puppy/

Dog Time Staff. (2010, August 18). The best way to clean up after your dog's house-soiling accidents. *Dog Time*. https://dogtime.com/how-to/home-cleaning/3485-the-best-way-to-clean-up-after-your-dog-s-house-soiling-accidents

DOGUE Staff. (2019, June 18). 10 commands to teach your dog. *DOGUE*.

https://dogue.com.au/club-dogue/posts/10-commands-to-teach-your-dog/

Donovan, L. (2019a, August 30). Leash train your puppy in 5 easy steps. *American Kennel Club.* https://www.akc.org/expert-advice/training/teach-puppy-walk-leash/

Donovan, L. (2019b, October 31). Puppy socialization: How to socialize a puppy. *American Kennel Club.* https://www.akc.org/expert-advice/training/puppy-socialization/

Duno, S. (2022, July 4). Are you making these puppy training mistakes? *Modern Dog Magazine.* https://moderndogmagazine.com/puppytraining

Esser, N. (2020, January 14). Puppy proofing. *OC Service Dogs.* https://ocservicedogs.com/new-blog/2020/1/14/puppy-proofing

Farricelli, A. (2022, April 14). Signs your puppy needs to go potty. *Pet Helpful.* https://pethelpful.com/dogs/Signs-Your-Dog-Need-to-Go-Potty

Flowers, G. (2017, August 31). *Reward and discipline during potty training. The Times.* https://www.shreveporttimes.com/story/life/columnists/gregg-flowers/2015/09/01/reward-discipline-potty-training/71341486/

Gallagher, A. (2013, August 20). 6 tips for choosing healthy puppy food. *PetMD.*

https://www.petmd.com/dog/centers/nutritio n/slideshows/tips-for-choosing-puppy-food#slide-2

Gibeault, S. (2020, December 23). How to stop your dog from jumping up on people. *American Kennel Club.* https://www.akc.org/expert-advice/training/how-to-stop-your-dog-from-jumping-up-on-people/

Good Boy Staff. (2022, July 4). Surviving the first 24 hours with your new puppy. *Good Boy.* https://www.goodboy.co.uk/advice-hub/surviving-the-first-24-hours-with-your-new-puppy/#:~:text=It%27s%20a%20good%20ide a%20to

Hembery, S. (2019, March 11). The amazing tale of hero dog swansea jack who saved 27 lives. *WalesOnline.* https://www.walesonline.co.uk/news/wales-news/amazing-tale-hero-dog-swansea-15954212

Hills Staff. (2016, March 4). Tips for potty training your new puppy. *Hill's Pet Nutrition.* https://www.hillspet.com/dog-care/training/puppy-potty-training-tips#:~:text=Calmly%20Address%20Accidents

Hollis, L. (2018, March 8). Potty training praise for puppies. *Daily Puppy.* https://www.dailypuppy.com/potty-training-praise-puppies-1020.html

Its a Dogs World Staff. (2022, July 4). Housebreaking. *Its a Dogs World.* https://www.itsadogsworld.biz/resources/articles/housebreaking/#:~:text=Try%20to%20feed%20at%20the

Jessica. (2018, April 16). How much time do I need for a dog? *Pawshake.* https://www.pawshake.com.au/blog/how-much-time-do-i-need-dog

Joyner, L. (2021, March 15). 6 ways to train your dog not to bite. *Country Living.* https://www.countryliving.com/uk/wildlife/pets/a35820366/stop-dog-biting/

K9 of Mine Staff. (2018, April 1). *5 best dog proof trash cans: Keeping your dog out of garbage! K9 of Mine.* https://www.k9ofmine.com/dog-proof-trash-can/#:~:text=The%20silent%20close%20lid%20helps

Karetnick, J. (2022, March 19). Best dog beds: How to choose the comfiest bed for your pup. *American Kennel Club.* https://www.akc.org/expert-advice/lifestyle/best-dog-beds-choose-comfiest-bed-pup/#:~:text=To%20find%20the%20ideal%20dog

Kaufmann's Puppy Training Staff. (2016, November 20). How to potty train a puppy fast: The ultimate guide. *Kaufmann's Puppy Training.* https://kaufmannspuppytraining.com/en/how-to-potty-train-a-puppy-fast/

Kelley, R. (2022, July 5). How nutrition supports trainability in your sporting. *Eukanuba Sporting Dog.* https://www.eukanubasportingdog.com/health -and-nutrition/how-nutrition-promotes-trainability-in-puppies

Knapp, C. (2010). Caroline knapp quote. *Lib Quotes.* https://libquotes.com/caroline-knapp/quote/lbp6x0j

Kurtz, T. (2019, November 28). How to prevent a dog from chewing electrical cords. *The Dog People by Rover.* https://www.rover.com/blog/how-to-prevent-a-dog-from-chewing-electrical-cords/

Lowrey, S. (2021, May 13). Dog bell training: Teach a dog to ring bell to go outside. *American Kennel Club.* https://www.akc.org/expert-advice/advice/teach-dog-ring-bell-go-outside/

LTHQ Staff. (2019, October 13). How to use a crate to house train a puppy. *Labrador Training.* https://www.labradortraininghq.com/labrador-training/how-to-use-a-crate-to-house-train-a-puppy/#Crate_Your_Puppy_Around_Their_R egular_Toilet_Times

Mackin, C. (2022). It's easier to steer than stop a dog. *Pinterest.* https://za.pinterest.com/pin/73296090811470 0615/

Marie, J. (2019, October 8). Leaving dogs in a car: Is it too hot or cold? *Hill's Pet Nutrition.*

https://www.hillspet.com/dog-care/routine-care/leaving-dogs-in-hot-or-cold-cars#:~:text=On%20a%20mild%20day%20of

Martin, N. (2021, November 18). The 12 best dog gates and playpens for dogs. *The Dog People by Rover*. https://www.rover.com/blog/reviews/dog-gates/

Mattinson, P. (2018, September 11). Puppy potty training schedule with examples for pups of different ages. *The Happy Puppy Site*. https://thehappypuppysite.com/puppy-potty-training-schedule/

Mauran, C. (2022, May 15). How to clean up accidents according to seasoned pet owners. *Mashable*. https://mashable.com/article/how-to-clean-pet-stains-odors

Mearns, A. (2018, July 8). The d-backs honored a dog named todd, who saved his owner from a rattlesnake bite. *MLB Net*. https://www.mlb.com/cut4/diamondbacks-honor-dog-who-saved-owner-from-rattlesnake-c284839900#:~:text=On%20Friday%2C%20June%2029%2C%20Todd

Menteith, C. (2022, July 4). Get your puppy's first day home right. *Purina*. https://www.purina.co.uk/articles/dogs/puppy/welcoming/puppys-first-day-home#:~:text=Take%20things%20slowly%20on%20your%20puppy%27s%20first%20day%20home

Mitrokostas, S. (2020, April 6). Veterinarians share 10 things you should never do to your dog. *Insider.* https://www.insider.com/things-you-should-never-do-to-a-dog

Murphy, K. (2018, September 6). How to leash train a puppy. *Hill's Pet Nutrition.* https://www.hillspet.com/dog-care/training/leash-training-puppy

NBC News Staff. (2006, May 20). Dog makes cell phone call to save owner's life. *NBC News.* https://www.nbcnews.com/health/health-news/dog-makes-cell-phone-call-save-owners-life-flna1c9444411

Nelson, M. (2022, February 7). 3 ways to select a dog bed. *Wiki How.* https://www.wikihow.com/Select-a-Dog-Bed

Neumann, T. (2022, July 4). Dozer the dog runs solo maryland half marathon. *ESPN.* http://www.espn.com/espn/page2/index/_/id/6567417

NIH News in Health Staff. (2018, February 1). The power of pets. *NIH News in Health.* https://newsinhealth.nih.gov/2018/02/power-pets#:~:text=Possible%20Health%20Effects&text=Interacting%20with%20animals%20has%20been

Painter, S. (2022, January 31). *Potty training your puppy when you live in an apartment. Preventive Vet.*

https://www.preventivevet.com/dogs/potty-training-in-an-apartment

Parks, S. (2018, July 17). The secret to communicating with your dog so they really understand. *The Dog People by Rover.* https://www.rover.com/blog/how-to-communicate-dog-so-they-understand/

Parks, S., & Johnson, K. (2021, June 28). 16 tools you need to groom your dog at home, according to professional groomers. *Insider.* https://www.insider.com/guides/pets/best-dog-grooming-supplies

Perten, K. (2021, July 31). New puppy? These are the crates that vets & trainers recommend. *Bustle.* https://www.bustle.com/life/best-puppy-crates

Petco Staff. (2022, July 4). Picking the right type and size crate for your dog. *Petco.* https://www.petco.com/content/petco/Petco Store/en_US/pet-services/resource-center/home-habitat/select-the-right-crate-for-your-dog-wire-plastic-wood-and-more.html#:~:text=When%20figuring%20out%20how%20large

PetMD Staff. (2011, April 7). How to help prevent accidents during new puppy potty training. *PetMD.* https://www.petmd.com/dog/puppycenter/potty-training/evr_dg_how_to_prevent_puppy_accidents

PetMD Staff. (2017, January 13). Your new puppy: The ultimate puppy sleeping guide. *PetMD*. https://www.petmd.com/dog/care/your-new-puppy-ultimate-sleep-guide

Pevny, L. (2019, June 5). Does rubbing your dog's nose in their own poop or pee... really work? - little dog tips. *Little Dog Tips*. https://littledogtips.com/does-rubbing-your-dogs-nose-in-their-own-poop-or-pee-really-work/

Plymouth Veterinary Hospital Staff. (2020, June 11). Puppy flea and tick prevention. *Plymouth Veterinary Hospital*. https://www.plymouthvet.com/services/dogs/puppy-flea-and-tick-prevention#:~:text=Once%20your%20puppy%20is%20old

PupLife Staff. (2022, July 4). How to choose the right dog toys for your pet. PupLife Dog Supplies. https://www.puplife.com/pages/choosing-the-right-dog-toys-for-your-pet#:~:text=Make%20Sure%20They%20Are%20The

Puppy Leaks Staff. (2021, June 24). 10 ways to bond with your new dog. *Puppy Leaks*. https://www.puppyleaks.com/bond-with-new-dog/

PuppyTutor. (2017, October 12). What's the best gear for dog walking? *Puppy Tutor Dog Training*. https://puppytutor.me/best-dog-walking-gear/

Reisen, J. (2020, January 28). Bringing a puppy home: Help your puppy adjust to a new home. *American Kennel Club*. https://www.akc.org/expert-advice/training/8-tips-to-help-your-new-puppy-adjust-to-new-home/

Reisen, J. (2021, August 30). *Losing patience with puppy? How to have patience with a puppy*. *American Kennel Club*. https://www.akc.org/expert-advice/training/how-to-be-patient-with-your-new-puppy/

Reshareworthy Editorial Team. (2015, November 12). Military dog who saved thousands of lives and faced euthanasia gets a hero's welcome home. *Reshareworthy*. https://www.reshareworthy.com/mwd-dexter-welcome-home/

Ro, L. (2021, August 17). What pet owners need to clean and protect their furniture. *The Strategist*. https://nymag.com/strategist/article/best-pet-safe-cleaning-products-for-pet-messes.html

Rosenberg, K. (2022, May 12). How to stop your puppy crying in crate and help them settle. *Pets Radar*. https://www.petsradar.com/advice/how-to-stop-a-puppy-crying-in-crate

Ross, A., Smedema, D., Parada, F. J., & Allen, C. (2014, February). Visual attention in dogs and the evolution of non-verbal communication. *ResearchGate*. https://www.researchgate.net/publication/285

947442_Visual_Attention_in_Dogs_and_the_E
volution_of_Non-Verbal_Communication

Rowan, C. (2022, April 28). Is my dog happy? *PetMD*.
https://www.petmd.com/dog/behavior/is-my-
dog-
happy#:~:text=Relaxed%20or%20Wiggly%20B
ody%20and

Royal Canin Staff. (2018, March 10). How to introduce
a new puppy? *Royal Canin*.
https://www.royalcanin.com/us/dogs/puppy/i
ntroducing-your-puppy-to-family-members

Ryan, S. (2016, May 2). Crate and relaxation training for
dogs and puppies. *Developing Dogs*.
https://www.developingdogs.co.uk/crate-and-
relaxation-training-for-dogs-and-
puppies/#:~:text=Gradually%20increase%20th
e%20delay%20between

Schulz, C. M. (2010). A quote by Charles M. Schulz.
Goodreads.
https://www.goodreads.com/quotes/1025-
happiness-is-a-warm-puppy

Seidl, F., Levis, N. A., Jones, C. D., Monroy-Eklund,
A., Ehrenreich, I. M., & Pfennig, K. S. (2019).
Variation in hybrid gene expression:
Implications for the evolution of genetic
incompatibilities in interbreeding species.
Molecular Ecology, 28(20), 4667–4679.
https://doi.org/10.1111/mec.15246

Sharpe, S. (2021, November 5). *How to crate train your dog in 9 easy steps. American Kennel Club.* https://www.akc.org/expert-advice/training/how-to-crate-train-your-dog-in-9-easy-steps/

Sheaffer, S. (2022, January 11). How to know if your dog is confident. *USA Dog Behavior, LLC.* https://www.usadogbehavior.com/blog/2022-1-11-how-to-know-if-your-dog-is-confident

Shibashake. (2022, April 21). Dog discipline: Does hitting and beating a dog work? *Pet Helpful.* https://pethelpful.com/dogs/An-Ear-for-an-Ear-Why-Biting-your-Dogs-Ear-Does-not-Work-aversive-techniques-forceful-punishment-do-not-work

Shojai, A. (2022, March 24). Use dog language to communicate with your puppy. *The Spruce Pets.* https://www.thesprucepets.com/how-to-talk-to-puppies-dogs-2804572

Sit Means Sit Staff. (2011, April 20). How to tell if a dog is being aggressive. *Sit Means Sit.* https://sitmeanssit.com/dog-training-mu/austin-dog-training/how-to-tell-if-a-dog-is-being-aggressive/#:~:text=The%20signs%20of%20a%20dominant

Stregowski, J. (2021, June 31). How much does it really cost to own a dog? *The Spruce Pets.* https://www.thesprucepets.com/the-cost-of-dog-ownership-1117321

Sundstrom, K. (2015, September 30). The pros and cons of purebred dogs. *Care Resources.* https://www.care.com/c/the-pros-and-cons-of-purebred-dogs/

Tarver, M. (2006, June 19). Beagle honored as lifesaver. *Wtsp.* https://www.wtsp.com/article/news/beagle-honored-as-lifesaver/67-396325096

The Dog People by Rover Staff. (2015, October 27). 8 tips to socialize your dog with other dogs and humans. *The Dog People by Rover.* https://www.rover.com/blog/how-to-socialize-dog/

The Puppy Academy Staff. (2022, May 31). How to teach your puppy to walk on a leash! *The Puppy Academy.* https://www.thepuppyacademy.com/blog/2020/8/17/teach-your-puppy-to-walk-on-a-leash

Toussaint, K. (2015, June 23). This blind terrier has his own seeing-eye dog and they're best friends. *Boston.com.* https://www.boston.com/culture/animals/2015/06/23/this-blind-terrier-has-his-own-seeing-eye-dog-and-theyre-best-friends/

Tractive Staff. (2022, February 7). Best 5 tips on how to leave your dog home alone without feeling guilty. *Tractive Blog.* https://tractive.com/blog/en/good-to-know/tips-for-leaving-your-dog-home-alone

Ulbrich, B. (2021, August 26). How to potty train a puppy in an apartment: 10 steps. *Wiki How*. https://www.wikihow.com/Potty-Train-a-Puppy-in-an-Apartment

University of Arizona. (2019). Do bigger brains equal smarter dogs? New study offers answers. *ScienceDaily*. https://www.sciencedaily.com/releases/2019/01/190129093722.htm

Unknown. (2020, September 28). 35+ dog training quotes: Inspirational & educational sayings. *Hepper*. https://www.hepper.com/dog-training-quotes/

WAH Staff. (2018, February 26). 10 houseplants that are dangerous for your dog. *Weddington Animal Hospital*. https://www.weddingtonanimalhospital.com/10-houseplants-that-are-dangerous-for-your-dog/

Waka Flocka Flame. (2020, January 8). No matter how youre feeling a little dog gonna love you. *365 Quotes*. https://365quotes.in/no-matter-how-youre-feeling-a-little-dog-gonna-love-you-waka-flocka-flame/

Walker, J. (2017, July 11). How to puppy-proof your house, especially the bathroom | coops and cages. *Coops and Cages*. https://www.coopsandcages.com.au/blog/puppy-proof-house-especially-bathroom/

Walsh, F. (2009). Human-Animal bonds I: The relational significance of companion animals. *ResearchGate*.
https://www.researchgate.net/publication/400 23863_Human-
Animal_Bonds_I_The_Relational_Significance_ of_Companion_Animals

Wikipedia Staff. (2021, January 27). Barry (dog). *Wikipedia*.
https://en.wikipedia.org/wiki/Barry_(dog)

Yordy, J., Kraus, C., Hayward, J. J., & White, M. (2020, February). Body size, inbreeding, and lifespan in domestic dogs. *ResearchGate*.
https://www.researchgate.net/publication/337 952753_Body_size_inbreeding_and_lifespan_in _domestic_dogs

Your Storage Finder Staff. (2022, July 4). Storing chemicals and allergens safely for your pets. *Your Storage Finder*.
https://www.yourstoragefinder.com/storing-chemicals-and-allergens-safely-for-your-pets

Made in the USA
Monee, IL
26 November 2024

70668549R00105